Toward a Framework for Financial Stability

Prepared by a Staff Team led by
David Folkerts-Landau and Carl-Johan Lindgren

INTERNATIONAL MONETARY FUND
Washington, DC
January 1998

BLI 2194-4/1

Library of Congress Cataloging-in-Publication Data

Toward a framework for financial stability / prepared by a staff team of
the International Monetary Fund led by David Folkerts-Landau and
Carl-Johan Lindgren.
    p. cm. — Includes bibliographical references

    ISBN 1-55775-706-2
    ISSN 0258-7440

    1. Monetary policy. 2. Economic stabilization. 3. Banks and
banking. I. Folkerts-Landau, D. F. I. (David Fokke Ihno), 1949-
II. Lindgren, Carl-Johan. III. International Monetary Fund.

HC230.3.T677 1998
332.4'6—dc21

                97-53266
                CIP

Price: US$25.00
(US$20.00 to full-time faculty members and
students at universities and colleges)

Please send orders to:
International Monetary Fund, Publication Services
700 19th Street, N.W., Washington, D.C. 20431, U.S.A.
Tel.: (202) 623-7430   Telefax: (202) 623-7201
E-mail: publications@imf.org
Internet:http://www.imf.org

recycled paper

Contents

	Page
Preface	**vii**
I. Introduction	**1**
II. Role of the IMF in Promoting Financial Stability	**4**
Role in Promoting Macroeconomic Stability	4
Role in Disseminating and Adapting Best Practices	5
Synergy Between the Two Roles	5
III. Key Aspects of a Framework for a Sound Financial System	**7**
Raising the Competence and Integrity of Management	7
Increasing the Transparency of Banking	8
Realistic Valuation of Bank Assets	8
Public Disclosure	8
Prudential Reporting	9
Limiting Public Sector Distortions	9
Lender-of-Last-Resort Facilities	9
Deposit Insurance	10
Exit Policy	10
Controlling Risk Through Regulatory and Supervisory Oversight	10
Prudential Regulation	11
Prudential Supervision	12
Strengthening the Broader Structural Framework	13
Fostering National and International Supervisory Coordination	14
IV. Quality of Information, Supervisory Reporting, and Public Disclosure	**16**
Quality of Banking Data	16
Accounting and Valuation Rules	16
Problems with Bank Asset Valuation and Income Recognition	17
Information for Supervisors	19
Information to Evaluate Decision-Making Structures and Management	19
Information to Evaluate Risks	20
Information to Evaluate Profitability	23
Information to Assess Capital and Capital Adequacy	23
Information for Public Disclosure	23
Information on the Condition of the Bank	25
Information on Earnings	26
V. Public Sector Guarantees	**27**
Components of Financial Safety Nets	27
Lender of Last Resort	27
Deposit Insurance	28
Exit Policy	29
Conservatorship	30

VI. Prudential Regulation of Banking — 32

Bank Licensing — 32
  Management, Nonexecutive Board Members, and Shareholders — 33
  Business Plan — 34
Governance of Banks — 34
  Money Laundering — 35
  Internal Controls and Internal Audit — 35
  External Audits and Banking Supervision — 36
Quantitative Supervisory Tools — 36
  Capital Adequacy — 36
  Liquidity — 38
  Credit Diversification — 38
  Connected Lending — 39
  Foreign Exchange Exposure — 39
  Limits on Nonbank Activity — 39

VII. Supervisory Oversight — 41

Autonomy of Banking Supervision — 41
  Political Autonomy — 41
  Staffing and Resources — 42
  Immunities — 43
Powers of the Supervisory Authority — 43
Interaction with Other Financial Sector Supervisors and Law
  Enforcement Bodies — 44
Location of the Banking Supervision Function — 45
Off-Site Analysis and On-Site Inspections — 45
Remedial and Punitive Measures — 46

VIII. Cross-Border Supervision of Banks — 47

Evolution of Best Practices — 47
Current Status of Best Practices — 48
  Location of the Licensing and Lead Supervisory Authority — 48
  Licensing of Internationally Active Banks — 48
  International Implementation of Prudential Standards — 48
  Cross-Border Supervisory Information — 49
  Cross-Border Inspections — 49
  Supervisory Action Against Establishments Abroad — 49
  Information on Supervisory Systems and Structures — 50
  "Shell Banks" and Parallel-Owned Banks — 50
  International Financial Conglomerates — 50
  International Bank Liquidation — 51

Boxes

1. Market Risk-Measurement Systems — 22
2. Typical Practices for the Lender of Last Resort in Normal Times — 28
3. Typical Practices for a Successful Deposit Insurance Scheme Under Normal
  Conditions and in Systemic Crises — 30
4. Initial Capital — 33
5. Conglomerates — 35
6. The Basle Capital Accord — 37
7. The Basle "Standards" — 48

Annexes

   I.   Core Principles for Effective Banking Supervision   52

  II.   IOSCO Principles and Recommendations for the Regulation
           and Supervision of Securities Markets   72

References   **80**

The following symbols have been used throughout this volume:

. . .   to indicate that data are not available;

—   to indicate that the figure is zero or less than half the final digit shown, or that the item does not exist;

–   between years or months (for example, 1995–96 or January–June) to indicate the years or months covered, including the beginning and ending years or months;

/   between years (for example, 1995/96) to indicate a fiscal or financial year.

"Billion" means a thousand million; "trillion" means a thousand billion.

"Basis points" refer to hundredths of 1 percentage point (for example, 25 basis points are equivalent to ¼ of 1 percentage point).

"n.a." means not applicable.

Minor discrepancies between constituent figures and totals are due to rounding.

As used in this volume the term "country" does not in all cases refer to a territorial entity that is a state as understood by international law and practice. As used here, the term also covers some territorial entities that are not states but for which statistical data are maintained on a separate and independent basis.

Preface

Financial globalization and liberalization have heightened awareness of the crucial interrelationships between macroeconomic policy and financial sector developments. The Fund has thus placed greater emphasis on financial systems in its consultations, policy advice, and technical assistance. This paper was designed as a first step in designing a framework that could be used to further its work in the surveillance of its members' financial sectors. As such, it draws heavily on existing work, particularly that of the Basle Committee on Banking Supervision, which has greatly contributed to the promotion of internationally accepted standards and practices for bank supervision. To aid further dissemination, the recently published "Core Principles for Effective Banking Supervision" are annexed to this paper. In addition, the Fund is greatly indebted to the comments of a large number of experts, both members of the Basle Committee and supervisory officials from emerging market countries, as well as to a number of other commentators. The framework also benefits from the research of the Fund and the World Bank, as well as experience gathered by both institutions in providing technical assistance and policy advice to their member countries. The Fund also acknowledges the support of the International Organization of Securities Commissions for permission to annex some of its work.

The paper was prepared under the general direction of Manuel Guitián, Director of the Monetary and Exchange Affairs Department, and Michael Mussa, Economic Counselor and Director of the Research Department. It was written by a staff team headed by David Folkerts-Landau and Carl-Johan Lindgren and consisting of Donald Mathieson, Richard Abrams, Bankhim Chadha, Daniel Dueñas, Gillian Garcia, Jan Willem van der Vossen, Laura Kodres, Michael Spencer, Peter Hayward, and other staff of the Monetary and Exchange Affairs and Research Departments. Sheila Kinsella, Lisa Scott-Hill, Lidia Tokuda, and Adriana Vohden provided expert secretarial assistance. Marina Primorac edited the manuscript and coordinated the production of this publication.

The paper has benefited from comments and suggestions from staff in other IMF departments, as well as from Executive Directors following their discussion of an earlier draft of this paper on March 28, 1997. The analysis, however, is that of the contributing staff and should not be attributed to Executive Directors or their national authorities.

I

Introduction

It is now well recognized that vulnerable and unstable banking systems can severely disrupt macroeconomic performance in industrial, developing, and transition economies alike.[1] The widespread incidence and the high cost of banking problems have prompted calls for concerted international action to promote the soundness and stability of banking systems. At the Lyon Summit in June 1996, the Group of Seven (G-7) industrial countries called for "the adoption of strong prudential standards in emerging market economies," and encouraged the international financial institutions to "increase their efforts to promote effective supervisory structures in these economies."[2] These intentions were reinforced by the IMF Interim Committee's "Partnership for Sustainable Global Growth" in September 1996 (see IMF, 1996). In Denver, in June 1997, the G-7 Ministers of Finance meeting considered a report by a Group of Ten (G-10) working party on financial stability in emerging market economies (G-10, 1997) and requested "the IMF and the World Bank to report to Finance Ministers next April on their efforts to strengthen the roles they play in encouraging emerging market economies to adopt the principles and guidelines identified by the supervisory community" (G-7, 1997). The G-7 Heads of Government then called "on the international financial institutions and the international regulatory bodies to fulfill their roles in assisting emerging market economies in strengthening their financial systems and prudential standards." The Heads of Government also welcomed "the IMF's progress in strengthening surveillance and promoting improved transparency. Increased attention to financial sector problems that could have significant macroeconomic implications, and to promoting good governance and transparency, will help prevent financial crises" (G-7, 1997).

International financial institutions and official groupings[3] are responding to these concerns in their respective work programs. The Basle Committee has been in the forefront of this effort with the release of its "Core Principles for Effective Banking Supervision." These principles have quickly become the focal point for the increased efforts to strengthen financial sectors around the world by providing a blueprint for enhanced banking supervision, and they provide the foundation for the framework described in this paper.

The IMF, with its near-universal membership, has an important role to play in this ongoing international effort. The IMF can help assure broad dissemination of the work of various organizations, particularly that of the Basle Committee. To this end, the "Core Principles" are attached to this paper as Annex I. Moreover, with its broad responsibility to engage in surveillance of member countries' economic policies, the IMF can assist in identifying potential vulnerabilities in the monetary and financial systems, and in the external positions of member countries, and it can help the authorities in formulating corrective policies.

The existing limitations on staff resources and expertise imply that an increase in IMF surveillance coverage of financial sector issues—as part of its ongoing bilateral or multilateral surveillance activities—will focus on identifying those weaknesses in the financial systems, particularly in the banking systems, of member countries that could potentially have major macroeconomic implications. Fund surveillance cannot be expected to address all the areas in the financial system that are in need of improvement, nor can it be expected to provide specific assistance to the regulatory and supervisory authorities in meeting their day-to-day challenges. Furthermore, in many member countries, banks remain the principal financial intermediaries for allocating and pricing credit and financial risk and for making payments, as well as being the main source of financial leverage. Hence, the IMF's efforts to enhance its work on financial system soundness will focus on the banking system, although attention will also need to be paid to those parts of the rest of the financial system that are potential sources of major difficulties.

Fund surveillance over banking sector issues of macroeconomic significance, and staff discussions on appropriate remedial measures with the authorities, will be enhanced and facilitated by a general statement of the broad principles and characteristics of sta-

---

[1]These issues have been extensively discussed elsewhere. See Lindgren, Garcia, and Saal (1996), and Folkerts-Landau and Ito (1995 and 1996).

[2]G-7 (1996).

[3]The Bank for International Settlements (BIS), the Basle Committee on Banking Supervision, the International Organization of Securities Commissions (IOSCO), the International Association of Insurance Supervisors (IAIS), the Group of Ten Deputies, the World Bank, regional supervisory groupings, and the IMF.

ble and sound financial systems. This paper suggests such a general framework, based on a generally agreed body of knowledge and experience. The application of this framework to individual countries will, of course, require careful consideration of country-specific circumstances as member countries' priorities for attainment of best practices will be different, based on their different traditions, existing structures, and resource constraints.

This framework is not a checklist of issues to be raised in each of the IMF's (usually annual) consultations with member countries under Article IV of its Articles of Agreement. Rather, it is intended to suggest broad categories of issues—and some detailed points within those categories—of particular importance for the discussion of financial sector issues of potential macroeconomic importance. Furthermore, consideration of issues in these broad categories, as part of the continuous process of Fund surveillance, can help identify circumstances where issues should be taken up with country authorities, sometimes on a more urgent basis than is permitted by the regular Article IV consultation schedule. Also, it is hoped that by promoting broader understanding of the requirements for sound banking and effective financial intermediation more generally, the development and promulgation of this framework—along with other similar efforts under way outside the Fund—may contribute to the general international effort to improve the soundness of financial systems, and thereby reduce the likelihood and diminish the intensity of future financial sector problems.

A number of official and industry groupings have for some time been compiling best practices, and formulating principles and guidelines, for use in the relevant sectors of the financial system.[4] The efforts of these groups, in particular those of the Basle Committee, have proved to be indispensable inputs into the formulation of the framework outlined in this paper.[5] As well as drawing on the work of the Basle Committee, the framework proposed in this paper has been developed in close consultation with the World Bank. The role of the World Bank in this area will complement and underpin the surveillance-oriented work of the Fund, in that its focus will fall on the microeconomic aspects of financial systems.

Although this paper describes in some detail the staff's distillation of widely accepted views on what constitutes such a framework for a sound and effective banking system, few, if any, of the Fund's members

have banking systems that possess all of these characteristics. The guidance provided here is mainly intended to assist in maintaining the soundness of relatively large and complex banking organizations—specifically, those that are internationally active. While some of the principles are applicable to all banks, a simpler structure may be sufficient for smaller and less complex institutions. The focus in this paper is on institutions that have the potential to create systemic problems domestically or internationally.

Furthermore, some countries have in place an effective framework for a sound banking system that differs from what is described here. Nevertheless, the paper can be seen both as providing guidance for the direction in which supervisory structures and financial system reforms should progress, and as indicating some measure of the policy challenges that lie ahead. As noted earlier, the focus is on the banking system, the main financial intermediary in most Fund member countries, although there are also nonbank financial intermediaries and other elements in the financial infrastructure that make important contributions to the soundness of the system as a whole.[6]

As emphasized in Chapter III, neither external market discipline nor supervisors alone can assure a safe and sound banking system. It is the appropriate combination of the two elements that encourages the competent and effective management that leads to a sound banking system. Alternatively, when managers have sufficient incentives, buttressed by market discipline, supervisors can use a lighter hand. It should be noted, however, that in many countries management needs external guidance, yet supervisors face political interference and have insufficient resources. Moreover, markets are embryonic. Thus, improvements are required in all relevant areas.

These principles and practices have been drawn from a wide spectrum of sources. The work of the Basle Committee on Banking Supervision on prudential standards as compiled in the Core Principles has been an important source. In addition, the technical assistance work of the Fund and the World Bank has yielded a wealth of insights into what constitutes sound banking.[7] Furthermore, the experiences of supervisory agencies in some of the major industrial and emerging market countries have been useful in identifying principles and best practices.

---

[4]See, for example, Annex II; the International Accounting Standards Committee (1997, 1994a, and 1994b); and Group of Thirty (1997).

[5]The Core Principles for Effective Banking Supervision (see Annex I), developed by a working group consisting of representatives of the Basle Committee and emerging market countries, have been a particularly important input.

[6]They include interbank payments and settlement systems; legal processes for the making and enforcing of contracts and the transfer of property, including the taking and perfecting of security for loans; and the workings of the judicial system so that banks have access to speedy and effective legal remedies. On payments systems see, for example, Folkerts-Landau et al. (1996).

[7]The Bank Supervision Guidelines issued by the World Bank (1992) and based on its extensive experience in advising countries on regulatory issues also have been an important influence on the development of best practices for prudential supervision in emerging markets.

Chapter II describes the role of the Fund in promoting financial stability as part of the ongoing broader international effort to achieve greater soundness in the financial systems of member countries. Chapter III describes the key aspects of the framework for a sound financial system discussed in more detail in subsequent chapters, that is, transparency of the financial system, public sector guarantees, prudential regulation, supervisory oversight, and supervision of cross-border banking.

Chapter IV examines the inherent difficulties encountered in compiling reliable and timely banking information. Best practices for the reporting of information to supervisors and for the disclosure of information to the public are described. Chapter V examines ways to limit the adverse impact on incentives that can arise when public sector guarantees and other official commitments are extended to bank depositors, creditors, and owners. There is a general consensus that safety nets need to be designed to work without unduly distorting the risk-taking behavior of bank stakeholders. The design of the components of a financial safety net—lender of last resort and deposit insurance arrangements—is discussed. The chapter suggests principles for the use of a strong exit policy for insolvent banks as a means to limit the extent of

official guarantees and undertakings. Chapter VI presents a framework for prudential regulation based on the premise that regulatory restrictions on the activities of banks are needed to counteract the adverse incentives for risk-taking created by public sector commitments. The chapter discusses licensing policy, various qualitative requirements to strengthen governance, and the design and structure of quantitative prudential regulations.

Chapter VII presents principles and practices of prudential banking supervision. The focus is on the autonomy, authority, and capacity of the supervisor. The interaction of the bank supervisory authority with other supervisory and legal enforcement bodies is examined. The chapter also discusses practices of off-site monitoring and on-site inspection, and corrective and punitive measures available to the supervisor. Finally, Chapter VIII examines issues related to the supervision of cross-border banking. The focus is on the modalities of supervising the international activities of banks and on international coordination and cooperation in developing banking supervisory standards. The topics covered in this chapter include the location of licensing and lead supervisory authorities, the licensing of internationally active banks, cross-border exchanges of information, inspections, and sanctions.

II

Role of the IMF in Promoting Financial Stability

Role in Promoting Macroeconomic Stability

The thrust of policy efforts to strengthen financial sector performance has to originate with national authorities. But the Fund and the international community at large have an important stake in the success of these efforts, because banking crises have macroeconomic consequences and may generate significant regional and international spillovers. As more countries remove remaining restrictions on their capital account transactions, and as banking and finance assumes a more regional and international dimension, the cross-border impact of banking system problems can be expected to increase as well. These considerations have motivated broad international interest in contributing to the effort to achieve greater stability in banking and financial systems around the world, culminating in the statement by G-7 Heads of Government in Denver. The Fund's efforts to support the initiatives of many of its members to strengthen their financial system policies through its surveillance, lending, and technical assistance activities should be seen as part of this larger international effort now under way, and the Fund's work will have to be in concert with the endeavors of this broader international initiative.

The Fund's main instruments for promoting financial sector soundness are bilateral and multilateral surveillance, conditional lending, and technical assistance. In its bilateral surveillance activities, the Fund seeks to improve the macroeconomic environment and policies through a regular dialogue with the authorities of member countries and through discussions by the Executive Board of the IMF staff's appraisal of macroeconomic performance and policies. Since a stable macroeconomic environment and a sustainable external position are necessary conditions for a sound and effective financial system, this effort contributes significantly to the stability of the financial sector. At the same time, since a sound banking system contributes to macroeconomic stability, a focus on banking sector issues is also appropriate for the assessment of macroeconomic and balance of payments policy.

By extending its analysis of the banking system and, where necessary, broader financial system issues, the Fund's bilateral surveillance effort will also make a contribution to the wider international efforts to achieve greater stability in banking systems. The framework suggested here is, inter alia, meant to provide the Fund's staff with a broad guide for analyzing banking system issues by identifying key areas of vulnerability. Furthermore, the framework could be helpful in defining areas where corrective policies are called for, and it could provide guidance for policy discussions with authorities. Use of a framework such as that outlined here could help to make the analysis and policy discussions more consistent and transparent across a wide spectrum of the Fund's membership—although the focus on financial sector issues will need to be selective and due regard will have to be paid to the circumstances of individual countries. The increased focus of the Fund's surveillance on the financial sector will necessarily have to identify problems that are of potential macroeconomic concern. There is a need to develop soundness indicators for the key prudential areas discussed in this framework, to complement the relevant macroeconomic indicators.

The framework is to provide a broad basis for IMF staff to consider a range of issues that may be important, particularly in helping to identify circumstances in which a preliminary assessment may suggest potential benefits from further exploration. In the end, however, Fund surveillance will not be able to certify financial systems as "sound," or even reliably identify all instances in which difficulties in the financial sector may become a major macroeconomic concern. Rather, the objective must be to increase the awareness of financial sector problems, their potential consequences, and their appropriate solutions in selective instances where they may become a major concern. In this regard, as mentioned above, the framework suggested in this paper is clearly not a checklist of issues to be explored in every Article IV consultation, nor is it a diagnostic tool that could allow an assessment of the financial position of individual banking systems.

In its multilateral financial surveillance exercise, which is considered by the Executive Board in its discussion of the International Capital Markets Report, the IMF assesses systemic developments and risks in the global financial system. Such multilateral surveillance also seeks to identify financial problems and risks that have a potential for spilling over regionally or internationally. In considering banking system developments in systemically significant countries, these surveillance activities could also benefit from the consistent application of a framework for sound banking, such as the one suggested in this paper.

In addition to increased surveillance, efforts to strengthen banking systems and to deal with outright banking problems or crises have become a regular feature of Fund-supported adjustment programs in some countries. The IMF has often assisted in identifying and diagnosing banking system problems, in helping design strategies for systemic reforms and bank restructuring, and in ensuring that such strategies are consistent with, and supported by, appropriate macroeconomic policies. In several instances, a Fund-supported program has been contingent on major banking sector reforms or systemic bank restructuring. Such programs have at times been coordinated with loans from the World Bank and regional development banks in support of financial sector reforms or individual or systemic bank restructuring.

Furthermore, IMF technical assistance has helped to strengthen the financial infrastructure of many countries through advice on basic central bank and banking legislation; improvements in monetary and fiscal management; foreign exchange, money, and government debt market development; improvements in monetary statistics; the design of payment systems and deposit insurance arrangements; the development of prudential regulations and supervisory capabilities, and in particular the entry and exit of banks; and strategies for systemic crisis management and bank restructuring. These efforts have been aimed mainly at developing countries and economies in transition, but have also involved a significant number of other member countries.

Role in Disseminating and Adapting Best Practices

An indispensable ingredient in the international efforts has been the work of the various multilateral official and industry groupings to compile principles, best practices, and guidelines covering the relevant financial activities or arrangements. Furthermore, the experience gained in some of the major industrial countries in formulating and implementing guidelines, standards, and best practices for use in the financial sector can be helpful to the relevant national authorities in a wider spectrum of the Fund's members, and can contribute to the harmonization of rules and practices internationally.[8] The most successful of these initiatives has been the work of the Basle Committee on Banking Supervision, which has, inter alia, agreed on standards for capital adequacy and cross-border supervision of internationally active banks from the G-10 countries. These standards have now

been successfully adopted (and in some cases adapted) by many emerging market countries and in numerous other countries as well, at least in form, if not always in substance. In cooperation with supervisors from emerging markets, the Basle Committee's Core Principles for Effective Banking Supervision are expected to be endorsed by a wide spectrum of non-G-10 countries. Regional groups of bank supervisors, supported by the Basle Committee, have been active in promoting harmonization and improvements in regulatory and supervisory practices and are expected to support that process. Furthermore, IOSCO is working on similar standards for the securities industry, and there are incipient efforts by IAIS for the insurance industry as well. In addition, the International Accounting Standards Committee is developing standards that are expected to be ready for international endorsement in March 1998. The standards, guidelines, or best practices being produced by these various expert groupings are crystallizing the experience gained over the past decade with formulating solutions to a wide array of problems in the financial system.

An increased focus on banking and financial sector issues by the IMF will contribute to the dissemination of best practices and will thus over time contribute to a harmonization of financial policies and practices internationally. At the same time, country experiences, as well as changing market conditions and other circumstances, will require that the framework suggested in this paper undergo regular revision. The experience that the IMF is gaining in its surveillance and technical assistance work can usefully be shared with the various expert groups. This suggests that cooperation and consultation between Fund staff and these groups are mutually beneficial.

Synergy Between the Two Roles

There is undisputed evidence that banking sector problems can be costly and disruptive to macroeconomic performance, and that the impact of such problems can make itself felt extensively across national borders. While national authorities have the primary responsibility for addressing banking problems, a concerted international effort, involving international financial institutions and expert groupings, is under way to reduce the incidence and cost of such problems.

The near-universal membership of the IMF and its mandate to promote macroeconomic and exchange stability suggest that the Fund is well placed to contribute to a strengthening of the financial systems in its members by enhancing its surveillance to cover developments in their banking systems, particularly where they exhibit problems with potential for generating serious macroeconomic disturbances. The continuous nature of the surveillance process is well

---

[8]See Goldstein (1996).

suited to monitor and support the sustained efforts required by national authorities to improve the soundness and the stability of banking systems in member countries. The conditionality applied to the use of the Fund's resources can be, and indeed has been, used to ensure that weaknesses in members' banking systems are dealt with in a timely and effective fashion. Finally, the IMF's extensive program of technical assistance can be used to ensure that member countries, in the process of liberalizing their banking systems, learn from the experience of others.

For the Fund's coverage of banking systems in its member countries to be as effective, consistent, and transparent as possible, it is desirable to have a framework of general principles of sound banking that can assist in the analysis and assessment of the performance of banking systems across the wide spectrum of the IMF's membership.

In arriving at an initial outline of such a framework, the IMF has drawn to the maximum extent possible on the ongoing work of various standard-setting international groupings. The efforts of the Fund to extend and strengthen its surveillance over the macroeconomic implications of the operation of banking systems builds on, and is consistent with, the work of these international groupings, and in particular the work of the Basle Committee in the specific area of bank supervision. In turn, the IMF's growing experience with surveillance over banking system issues can be used as input into the work of these groupings, and the Fund can help to adapt these standards and best practices to the varying circumstances of its wider membership.

III

Key Aspects of a Framework for a Sound Financial System

While not the subject of this paper, it must always be remembered that an unstable macroeconomic environment is a principal source of vulnerability in the financial system. Significant swings in the performance of the real economy, and volatile interest rates, exchange rates, asset prices, and inflation rates make it difficult for banks to assess accurately the credit and market risks they incur. Moreover, banks in many developing and transition economies have limited scope to diversify these risks as much as is possible in industrial economies. Large and volatile international capital flows often add to the challenges faced by banks in these countries. While Fund surveillance will seek to improve the macroeconomic framework, a structural framework for sound banking should also attempt to ensure that the macroeconomic risks are adequately reflected in prudential restraints and structural policies.

The second general source of vulnerability in the banking system, which is the focus of the framework for sound banking discussed in this paper, stems from weakness in the management of the banks themselves and in the structural environment in which they operate. Such weakness together with a poor incentive structure leads, inter alia, to excessive risk-taking, and undermine corporate governance and market discipline—fundamental ingredients for sound banking. For purposes of organizing the elements of a framework, five broad sets of challenges can be identified. First, inadequate bank management leads to undue risk-taking, to the detriment of the interests of depositors and other creditors. Second, a lack of adequate information on the financial condition of banks—due in part to inadequate accounting standards and reporting and disclosure requirements, but principally owing to insufficiently stringent rules and practices for loan valuation and loan loss provisioning—undermines the disciplining force of markets and delays recognition of banking problems until well after the onset of difficulties, thereby making their resolution harder and costlier. Third, the presence of implicit or explicit public sector guarantees of the liabilities of banks—the official safety net—in many cases has contributed to weakness in banking systems by encouraging excessive risk-taking by individual banks and weakening the discipline that would be imposed by depositors with money at risk. Forbearance in dealing with insolvent banks through a weak exit policy—in combination with generous support for depositors and extensive lender-of-last-resort assistance—frequently increases the ultimate costs of banking crises. Fourth, an ineffective bank supervisory environment frequently fails to counter the incentive problems created by the public sector safety net and by a lack of market discipline. Although most countries have elaborate regulatory systems, such systems often are not effectively implemented and enforced because of a lack of supervisory autonomy and capacity. Fifth, concentrated bank ownership and connected lending may increase the vulnerability of banking systems, particularly in developing countries. When banks are part of larger conglomerates, there is often a propensity for a significant portion of the lending of these banks to be directed to associated entities, making it difficult to evaluate the credit quality of loans and their collateral and to measure the origin and quality of a bank's capital. In addition, state ownership of banks is frequently associated with inadequate governance, extensive guarantees of bank liabilities, and lax implementation of supervisory requirements.

Raising the Competence and Integrity of Management

The first line of defense against unsound banking is competent management. Most bank failures can be attributed to inadequate management that allows the bank to acquire low-quality assets and take inappropriate risk positions and that fails to detect and resolve deterioration in existing assets and risk positions. Quantitative regulation, although important, cannot ensure that a bank is well run. Bank managements need to possess a high degree of integrity and have adequate training and experience to do the job. Sound management will ensure that good internal information and control systems are installed, for example to ensure that decisions affecting the rights and obligations of the bank never rest with just one individual (the "four eyes" principle). A sound bank will have prudent credit approval procedures, risk limitation, and administration procedures, which are well documented, and will appropriately delegate authority to the various levels of management.

Effective internal controls are necessary to ensure that established policies and procedures are followed and that special interests are not allowed to influence decisions. The bank's board needs to have effective control over the management, using internal and external audit procedures to satisfy itself, the shareholders, and the supervisory authority that the management is discharging its functions competently and in the interests of the bank as a whole. The board should also ensure a proper relationship between the bank and its proprietors as well as with the supervisory authority, avoiding conflicts of interest among these entities.

Increasing the Transparency of Banking

It is inherently difficult to obtain a reliable assessment of the financial condition of banks, since most bank assets are illiquid and lack an objectively determined market value. The estimated current value of banks' loan portfolios should be reflected in the size of loan loss provisions, but bank managers are often unable or unwilling to arrive at a realistic measure of banks' impaired loan portfolios. The incentives for underreporting or concealing data on bad loans grow as a bank's financial situation deteriorates. In addition, the growing internationalization of banks and the introduction of modern information technology by internationally active banks has enabled these institutions to rapidly move some of their risk positions into off-balance sheet or trust vehicles located on- and offshore. It has also become easier for banks to circumvent domestic prudential restraints on their risk exposures through the use of derivative products.[9] The ability of supervisors to monitor these activities has generally lagged behind the ability of banks to design new instruments.[10]

The opaqueness of banks' financial data is the Achilles' heel of effective corporate governance, market discipline, and official oversight in banking. External auditors and supervisors often fail to detect inflated loan values and inadequate provisioning. The monitoring of prudential ratios and restrictions on credit and market risk positions, including capital adequacy ratios, may thus become less effective as a means of detecting underlying problems. External auditors can play a useful role—in some countries a major role—but only where the profession is significantly skilled and has a direct reporting responsibility to the supervisor. Elsewhere, the only external agents generally in a position to assess the adequacy of

banks' loan provisioning with a significant degree of confidence are the bank supervisors themselves. Arriving at such an assessment is one of the most important aspects of bank supervision, and one that requires competent supervisors with authority to overrule the valuations of banks and auditors. Misreporting of basic bank balance sheet data distorts not only prudential analysis but also monetary and macroeconomic analysis. Furthermore, the lack of "hard" data tends to encourage supervisory forbearance and makes the supervisory and judicial processes more vulnerable to political influences.

Realistic Valuation of Bank Assets

Hence, an important component of a framework for sound banking is that the system produces timely and reliable information for use by management, supervisors, and market participants. To this end, it is desirable to support the introduction of internationally recognized accounting standards, including a broad application of principles for consolidation of the operations of financial groups or conglomerates. Particular attention will need to be paid to loan classification, provisioning, and income recognition rules, and to the practices for their effective implementation.[11] Accounting, valuation, provisioning, and consolidation rules need to be complemented by proper procedures and practices for their effective implementation. Banks, therefore, need to have adequate internal reporting and control procedures and, in particular, appropriate credit approval, monitoring, classification and valuation, and recovery procedures.

Public Disclosure

The more reliable and extensive the information that is disclosed by banks to the markets, the more effective is market discipline. However, the accuracy of public data on the performance of a bank often diminishes during times of stress. Indeed, the integrity of financial data is likely to deteriorate precisely at the time when it would be most needed, that is, when the bank is experiencing serious difficulties. Given these complications, best practices for disclosure in many countries typically go beyond disclosing traditional financial statements to include providing other quantitative and qualitative information, such as the struc-

---

[9]Although, when used prudently, derivatives enable banks to reduce their exposures and to manage risk better for the benefit of depositors as well as shareholders.

[10]See Folkerts-Landau and Garber (1997).

[11]Internationally agreed accounting practices special to banks have not yet obtained widespread official recognition. However, the International Accounting Standards Committee (IASC) is developing such standards. Two of the standards particularly relevant to banks are IAS 30 and 32; and the Basle Committee has established a task force to contribute to the process. A complete set of accounting standards developed by the IASC is available from the International Accounting Standards Committee, 167 Fleet Street, London, EC4A 2ES, United Kingdom.

ture of the bank's ownership, risk concentration, and details of policies and practices of risk-management systems.[12] Rating agencies can contribute to improving the transparency of banking data by demanding increased disclosure as a precondition for a rating.

Prudential Reporting

Banks are required to report directly to supervisors, normally on the same basis as is disclosed to the public, but such reporting would include details of specific risks whose public disclosure would be unwelcome to individual customers as well as being market sensitive. It is generally acknowledged that supervisors should have the right to request all relevant data from banks at reasonable notice. Supervisory reporting requirements and associated off-site monitoring typically encompass both quantitative and qualitative bank-specific information that can be used to assess the risks that banks face (including weaknesses in their loan portfolios), the ability of managers to control risks, and the performance of the banking system as a whole. Qualitative information generally encompasses such items as credit policies, investment and trading strategies, the mechanisms of internal controls, the affiliations of major bank shareholders or senior management, and changes in corporate structure. Supervisors in the major financial centers increasingly focus on the adequacy of the internal risk-control capabilities of banks. Quantitative information typically includes data on balance sheet and off–balance sheet items, and reports on earnings, loan concentration, maturity and foreign exchange exposures. Not surprisingly, the greatest problems of reporting have been associated with loan valuation and (its mirror image) capital adequacy, and with offshore activities.

Limiting Public Sector Distortions

If markets are to play an important role in disciplining bank managers and owners, there must be a presumption that financial assistance will not be provided automatically to troubled banks, and that owners and large creditors will not be fully protected. This suggests that, as a general principle, banks that are deemed to be insolvent by supervisors should be forced to exit in a timely manner, to prevent problems in individual banks from growing and contaminating other banks. Recent experience in a large number of IMF member countries suggests that public sector support for failing banking institutions is generally

unduly broad. While the danger of precipitating a general loss of confidence has frequently made it difficult to close large banks without fully compensating most depositors, it is almost always possible to make the owners and large creditors bear a substantial part of the financial burden of losses. Such a prospect enhances the incentives for large and relatively well-informed creditors, including other banks, to exercise market discipline on weaker banks, not only because large creditors have more resources with which to monitor and influence individual banks, but also because they typically have access to better information than anyone else. The broad goal for public sector policy is to leave enough room for markets to work sufficiently well that the banks' funding cost will appropriately reflect the quality of their balance sheets.

In countries where directed lending and other quasi-fiscal operations involving banks, including different types of guarantees, conceal government subsidies and transfers, it is difficult for the government to deny support to these institutions when they run into difficulties. When such quasi-fiscal operations are being used, they are more effective when fiscal authorities transparently record and present the cost of such operations in the budget. Furthermore, if the tax regime is not to discourage prudent banking, banks must receive the benefit of a lower tax liability in making required loan loss provisions.[13] Moves to limit such quasi-fiscal operations and to reduce such adverse incentives introduced by the tax system can make an important contribution toward sounder banking.

The framework of limited financial safety nets and strict bank exit policy described below is applicable to individual banks in relatively sound banking systems. If the entire banking system is in distress it may not be possible to apply bank-specific principles, but instead system-wide restructuring strategies may well be needed (see Alexander et al., 1997; and Lindgren, Garcia, and Kiyei, forthcoming).

Lender-of-Last-Resort Facilities

The proper role of central bank lender-of-last-resort facilities[14] is to promptly provide temporary support to illiquid but solvent institutions, typically at a penalty rate and against collateral, and to deny support to insolvent banks. Such lending can be an important instrument to prevent banking panics and runs that could cause sound institutions to become illiquid

---

[12]Chapter IV discusses what information is made available in countries that follow the International Accounting Standards and the most recent European Union and Euro-currency Standing Committee recommendations.

[13]See the discussion of loan loss provisioning in Chapter IV.

[14]Lender-of-last-resort facilities for banks, when they exist, are typically provided by the central bank as part of its role in assuring adequate liquidity in financial markets generally, but can also be provided by other public sector entities, such as state-owned banks, public sector enterprises, and pension schemes (depositing funds in troubled banks).

and precipitate their insolvency. In practice, however, such lending has often supported insolvent banks—allowing them to stay in business and compete with solvent banks—thus undermining market discipline and the profitability of the banking system. Such behavior by central banks usually reflects concern about precipitating a crisis of confidence in the banking system that is already generally weak, often due to adverse macroeconomic conditions as well as weak bank management.[15] Also, the data problems discussed above make it difficult to distinguish illiquid but solvent from insolvent institutions. And there is frequently hope that the institution will work its way out of trouble.

In order for a lender of last resort to operate effectively, without undermining market discipline, it needs to have sufficient information from the supervisory authority to determine which banks are approaching insolvency, to be able to limit support to sound but liquidity-constrained institutions, leaving the support of insolvent institutions to the fiscal authorities as soon as they can be identified.[16] This points again to the importance of good banking data.

Deposit Insurance

Deposit insurance arrangements are designed to compensate some classes of depositors in case of individual bank failures. However, deposit insurance schemes are prone to problems of moral hazard and need to be designed to contain such problems (see Lindgren, Garcia, and Kiyei, forthcoming; and Garcia, 1996). Most effective schemes are therefore limited to protecting small depositors and do not cover large depositors and other creditors, including other banks, so as to create incentives for market discipline to exert pressure on banks. The breadth of insurance coverage may vary depending on country-specific circumstances, but would remain subject to the constraint of containing moral hazard.

A deposit insurance system needs to be well funded so that it has the resources to pay off insured depositors promptly and allow the expeditious closure of insolvent members. As far as possible, the system should be self-financing. Insurance fees need to be high enough to cover the insurance cost of individual bank failures. Although it is desirable for fees to vary according to the estimated risk the insurance fund assumes, in practice it is difficult to arrive at an objective measure of risk that can be used for this purpose

and, therefore, uniform premiums remain the most common form of pricing.

Exit Policy

A credible exit policy for problem banks is necessary for effective deposit insurance and lender-of-last-resort arrangements, and for the maintenance of a sound and competitive banking system. For exit to occur smoothly, the financial system must be sufficiently robust to limit the spillovers from the failing institution to the rest of the system. It is, therefore, desirable that banks be closed before they become deeply insolvent and cause major losses for their creditors. But even when these conditions are satisfied, the modalities of winding up a bank of significant size, whether through a merger, breakup, or closure, generally require intervention by the supervisory authority, rather than simple application of the general bankruptcy statutes.

To reduce the scope for political pressure to prevent the exit of a bank, it may be helpful to limit supervisory discretion in favor of rule-based policies in the form of arrangements requiring prompt corrective action.[17] In this case, the supervisory authority is required to force the bank to undertake remedial action well before it reaches the point of negative net worth. However, to be effective, a policy of prompt corrective action requires timely and reliable information. In general, bank closures require a strong supportive legal framework, and rapid official intervention requires that supervisors have the authority to act outside the standard corporate bankruptcy procedures and without the need for political approval on a case-by-case basis.

Controlling Risk Through Regulatory and Supervisory Oversight

Regulation and supervision of banks seek to limit the adverse impact of the official safety net on risk-taking and to force banks to internalize the externalities of failures.[18] The objective of such oversight should not be to guarantee the survival of every bank, but rather to make sure that the banking system as a whole remains sound. As discussed above, such oversight should result in the exit of insolvent banks when market discipline fails. The supervision of individual

---

[15]Banks typically become insolvent before becoming illiquid and the position of banks reporting near-insolvency often turns out to be much worse once their true condition becomes apparent in the course of official intervention.

[16]If the government would like to provide solvency support for individual banks, this should be done in a transparent manner through the national budget.

[17]For a detailed description of such schemes, see Chapter V.

[18]See, for example, the remarks by Chairman Alan Greenspan at the meeting of the Institute of International Finance, Washington, April 29, 1997: "The presence of the safety net, which inevitably imparts a subsidy to banks, has created a disconnect between risk-taking by banks and banks' cost of capital. It is this disconnect that has made necessary a degree of supervision and regulation that would not be necessary without the existence of the safety net."

banks is, of course, the responsibility of the national supervisory authority and is not an area that Fund surveillance would normally cover; nonetheless, there are cases in which inadequacy in the supervisory approach can be a cause of system weakness with macroeconomic consequences, thus making it a legitimate case of inquiry. The best practices discussed in this section, and further detailed in Chapter VII, are largely based on the Core Principles for Effective Banking Supervision developed by the Basle Committee in consultation with supervisors from emerging market economies.

Prudential Regulation

Banking laws and prudential regulations seek to (1) establish policies that allow only financially viable banks to operate; (2) limit excessive risk-taking by owners and managers of banks; (3) establish appropriate accounting, valuation, and reporting rules; and (4) provide for corrective measures and restrictions on activities of weak institutions. Banking laws typically leave implementation to be defined by prudential regulations, to permit flexibility as circumstances change. The responsibility for promulgating regulations is normally vested in the supervisory authority.

Appropriate entry policies are essential for prudent banking and for healthy competition in the banking market. Financial sector liberalization often leads to calls for market entry, but an excessively lax entry policy often leads to banking problems at a later stage, particularly when the capacity of bank management and domestic supervisors is inadequate. Licenses may be granted only when prudential criteria are met. Entry policy not only has to address prudential issues, but also has to pay due regard to the capacity of the supervisory authority to execute its functions. It needs to strike a judicious balance between the objective of fostering competition (by encouraging entry) and maintaining supervisory effectiveness (by limiting entry).[19] This is best achieved if licensing is the responsibility of the supervisory authorities, and supervisors have authority to deny a license.[20] If a bank ceases to meet its licensing agreement, this then triggers corrective measures or becomes grounds for withdrawal of the license. Major changes in ownership or management also need to be subject to supervisory approval.

The licensing process attempts to ensure that a prospective banking enterprise will have suitably qualified owners and be properly organized, professionally managed, financially viable, and potentially profitable. The process is typically set out in the banking law and, inter alia, verifies whether (1) the initial capital is sufficient; (2) the major shareholders and management are suitable for their offices; (3) the corporate structure is transparent; (4) the bank's organizational structure, including the quality of its administrative and internal control systems, is adequate; and (5) in the case of a branch of a foreign bank, the bank is adequately supervised in its home country and the establishment of the branch is approved by the home country supervisor.

Capital adequacy ratios are viewed by the supervisory community as the most important restriction on banks' portfolio positions. The ratios are intended to ensure that banks maintain a minimum amount of own funds in relation to the risks they face, to absorb unexpected losses and give owners and managers an incentive to run banks safely. The most widely accepted method of measuring capital adequacy is the risk-weighted capital adequacy ratio promulgated by the Basle Committee (the Basle Capital Accord). Under this system, banks are required to hold different categories (tiers) of capital against assets and off-balance sheet items with different risk weights. This system was originally designed for internationally active G-10 banks, with good management and widely diversified risk portfolios. Supervisors in many other countries, where risk is more highly concentrated, management less experienced, and markets more volatile and less deep, and thus asset values more questionable, have concluded that ratios need to be considerably higher, and risk weights assigned to asset categories may need adjustment. Moreover, many international banks have found that to obtain the lowest funding rates, markets require a margin over the Basle minima. The Basle Committee has also developed an expanded system of capital adequacy ratios designed to incorporate market risks (foreign exchange, commodity, interest rate, and equity risk).[21] As mentioned above, effective measurement of capital adequacy requires proper valuation of banks' assets, and until this has been achieved, any analysis of capital adequacy ratios has to be undertaken with special caution. Moreover, capital adequacy ratios are often lagging indicators of banking problems and can be prone to manipulation through data problems.

---

[19]However, supervisors need to beware of self-serving arguments by existing banks that more competition would endanger the system.

[20]The Basle Committee's Core Principles envisage the possibility of a separate body responsible for licensing, in which case the supervisory authority must have the legal right to have its views considered by the licensing authority. In either case, the licensing criteria should be clear and objective and the process transparent.

[21]The option that supervisors allow banks to use their own in-house risk management systems to calculate market risk-based capital requirements is so far applicable only to banks in major money centers with special expertise.

Limits on excessive risk-taking seek to promote prudent banking by constraining lending concentration, lending to insiders, liquidity mismatches, and net foreign asset (or liability) positions.[22] Needless to say, the enforcement of these limits requires reliable information on a consolidated basis in order to be fully effective. Limits on risk concentration take different forms, but irrespective of their form, such limits seek to restrict exposure to a single borrower or connected group of borrowers or counterparties, to various sectors, and to market risk. Connected and insider lending to counterparties that are related to a bank, such as directors, managers, dominant shareholders, and their families, and lending to related corporate units, is best done on a nonpreferential basis and subject to tight limits, both individually and collectively.

Prudential liquidity regulations are imposed on banks in many countries to ensure that they are able to meet their creditor and depositor obligations without having to resort to forced asset sales or other costly means of raising funds.[23] Ensuring that there is not an excessive concentration of funding sources or a significant maturity mismatch between assets and liabilities helps limit the risks in banks' liability positions. Frequently, liquidity requirements do not remain true to their intended purpose and are used to create captive demand for short-term government obligations.

Constraints on managerial actions may restrict activities that have been associated with high-risk lending or investment activities that could expose banks to excessive risks. These constraints have been both restrictive and prescriptive, and apply in particular in cases where there are doubts that managers and owners continue to satisfy "fit and proper" criteria. Preferential treatment of insiders is restricted in order to minimize conflicts of interest. Prescriptive rules have included requirements that managers put in place adequate risk-management systems, including procedures for credit approval, monitoring, classification, and recovery, as well as for accounting, reporting, and internal audit functions.

Prudential regulations normally define accounting rules for banks to use in compiling their reports on income and financial condition to ensure consistency. Most important, such rules establish how banks value and classify loans, make provisions for loan losses, and suspend the accrual of overdue interest. They include criteria for the treatment of loan rollovers, refinancing, and other forms of "evergreening" where management manipulates lending practices to make loans appear to be performing when they are not.[24] It is the responsibility of bank management to implement these rules, while it is the responsibility of supervisors to ascertain that banks have the policies and procedures in place to ensure that the rules are applied appropriately. Examiners have the authority to force banks to reclassify loans, require additional provisions, and reverse inappropriately accrued interest, where necessary.

The supervisor often specifies additional responsibilities for external auditors, has access to external auditors' reports, and has the right to require the replacement of a bank's external auditors.[25] Such responsibilities in many cases oblige the external auditor to report material problems to the supervisor.

The supervisory agency is normally empowered by law to apply a range of corrective and punitive measures, when banks breach laws, prudential regulations, or licensing agreements. Supervisors need to be able to tailor their responses to be commensurate with the offense and gradually intensify the corrective measures.

Prudential Supervision

As part of their general duty to promote financial stability, banking supervisors monitor the soundness of the banking system, the adequacy of banks' risk-management practices and financial data, and their compliance with prudential regulations. To be effective, a supervisory authority must have sufficient autonomy, authority, and capacity. Supervisory autonomy, of course, needs to be combined with legal accountability, and involves freedom from political influences and adequate financial resources to meet supervisory objectives.

The autonomy issue is often linked with the location of the supervision function. In many countries the function is located in the central bank, sometimes with a separate board, while in some countries it is performed by an independent supervisory agency. There are arguments for and against locating the supervisory function in the central bank. On balance, at least in many emerging markets, the central bank appears to be the best location because it places the supervisor close to the central banks' other functions, such as lender of last resort, overseer of the payments system, and collector of macro-financial data. Moreover, supervisors can avail themselves of the authority, financial independence, and expertise of the central bank.

---

[22]Some supervisors prefer to exercise control by the imposition of capital requirements and by examination of the bank's own control systems rather than absolute limits. This applies particularly to liquidity and foreign exchange and other market risk positions.

[23]Although reserve requirements can also provide liquidity, they exist primarily for monetary policy purposes.

[24]In some developed markets, such rules are left to banks and auditors to devise, and the supervisor's role is to ensure that the rules are prudent and that banks adhere to them. But in most countries, supervisors have felt the need to play a more active role.

[25]In many countries where standards of bank auditing are not consistently high, supervisors maintain lists of approved auditors. Overt approval can, however, create an additional moral hazard for the supervisory authority if an approved auditor turns out to be deficient.

An effective supervisory authority has sufficient powers, established by law, to carry out its functions, including powers to control the issue and withdrawal of bank licenses, request relevant data, conduct on-site examinations in a bank and any of its branches and subsidiaries, verify the data supplied by banks, call for loan provisions, and restrain unsound practices, including issuing cease and desist orders and removing managers, denying or revoking licenses, and—where needed—forcing the exit of banks. In the absence of timely and reliable data, the authority of supervisors to use their own assessment of a bank's financial condition as a basis for corrective action is particularly important. Supervisory actions are often politically unpopular. Supervisors must, therefore, be able to act against banks without undue delays or pressures that result from a need for political approval or protracted court procedures.

Supervisors cover a range of increasingly sophisticated bank activities. They must not only verify banks' compliance with regulations and the accuracy of their reporting, but must also have the capacity to assess the suitability of the bank's owners and managers, the adequacy of loan valuation procedures and the banks' net worth, internal controls and audit procedures of banks, internal risk models, where applicable, and complex consolidated financial statements. In addition, they must be able to analyze relevant macroeconomic and market information, and take a view on behavior that may heighten systemic risk. To accomplish these increasingly demanding tasks, the supervisory authority should be able to attract and retain employees of high caliber and provide them with the necessary training, support, and appropriate remuneration.

Effective bank supervision must be seen by banks as a continuous presence. This is mainly achieved through off-site monitoring, both micro- and macroprudential in scope. Micro-prudential monitoring is based on quantitative and qualitative information reported by banks, and consists of verification of compliance with laws and prudential regulations, analysis of prudential ratios, and assessment of the individual bank's performance against peer groups and the entire industry. Macro-prudential analysis is based on market intelligence and macroeconomic information, and focuses on developments in important asset markets, other financial intermediaries, and macroeconomic developments and potential imbalances.

On-site inspections are needed to assess the adequacy of management and internal control procedures and to verify the accuracy of supervisory reporting. The latter is particularly important, given the potential weaknesses of loan valuation. While national practices differ, there are some common best practices. In particular, these practices call for all banks to be subject to some on-site inspection on a regular basis, and problem banks to be subject to particular scrutiny. Inspections should be comprehensive in scope and build on the inputs from the off-site monitoring. External auditors may play an important complementary role in banking oversight, but cannot replace supervisors. In some countries, on-site inspection is carried out by auditors acting under the specific instructions of the supervisory authority.[26]

Strengthening the Broader Structural Framework

The structure and concentration of ownership of the banking system may adversely affect the performance and stability of the system. Although there is a trend toward larger banks and financial conglomerates, such concentration increases the potential for systemic risk, which in turn increases the need for official oversight. Market perceptions that institutions are too big to fail will undermine market discipline and, therefore, require increased official supervision. Concentrated ownership has also meant that more focused political pressure can be exerted to obtain public sector guarantees for the liabilities of the bank. At the same time, in some developing countries the absence of a qualified controlling shareholder can result in ineffective oversight over management.

One of the issues relating to ownership concerns the desirability of state, private, or foreign ownership of banks. The track record of state-owned banks (including banks owned by central, state, and local governments) has frequently been poor. State-owned banks tend to bring competitive distortions to banking markets because they typically have access to low-cost capital and their liabilities tend to be fully guaranteed by the public sector. They are frequently exempted de jure or de facto from prudential requirements and have preferential access to deposits.[27] Nevertheless, there may be circumstances in which state-owned banks can operate effectively, if they are required to operate according to commercial criteria and conform to the same prudential rules as private banks, and if they fully and transparently transfer all their quasi-fiscal undertakings to the government budget. Since these conditions are rarely met in emerging market countries, privatization may be the best way to attain a sounder banking system.

Private ownership in itself is no guarantee for good governance. There may be countries in which no suit-

---

[26]Unlike external auditors, these firms normally report to, and in some cases are appointed and paid by, the supervisory authority. For such an arrangement to substitute adequately for traditional examiners, a reliable, skilled, and independent auditing profession is required.

[27]It should be noted that state-owned banks often are conduits for quasi-fiscal operations, which may then be used as justifications for forbearance from normal rules.

able private owners are available, in which case the state may be called upon to provide banking services; in such cases normal prudential banking criteria are best applied. In some countries the lack of a capital market and the concentration of wealth are such that banking interests cannot be kept apart from other economic or political interests, frequently leading to conglomerates that include a deposit-taking institution. In such cases it is important that the bank not be used as a captive source of finance by their owners, other insiders, or related enterprises.

Efficient banking systems are open to foreign ownership (through branches, subsidiaries, or partial ownerships), especially when there are only a few private domestic banks, to stimulate competition. Highly rated and adequately supervised foreign banks often bring necessary competition to inefficient domestic markets, and introduce professional skills and new technology. Perhaps most important, they typically reduce systemic risk because they tend not to be affected as readily by confidence problems as domestic institutions and they are less likely to make claims on the official safety net.

One problem that many countries face is the treatment of nonbank financial intermediaries. These fall into three categories. First, there are insurance, securities trading, and fund management businesses, which are normally regulated separately but increasingly are in common ownership with banks, giving rise to complex consolidated supervision problems. Second, there are finance companies, often owned by banks, sometimes created to avoid the full rigor of prudential, monetary, or tax regulations. Such institutions are often constrained by not being permitted to take deposits or use banking names, unless supervised as banks, but they may nevertheless depend on banks for funding and thereby create the potential for systemic risk. Finally, there are less reputable entities and activities, such as the "pyramid" schemes seen recently in a number of countries and other forms of deposit taking outside the books of licensed financial institutions. Here, there is a need for effective legal provisions to prevent the taking of deposits (or the use of banking names) by unauthorized entities or in unauthorized forms, together with a prosecuting authority that will respond to requests for action by the central bank and the supervisory authority.

Sound banking is facilitated by a strong financial market infrastructure, including an efficient payments system and money, as well as foreign exchange and capital, markets. In addition, the presence of institutional investors contributes to corporate governance. Payments systems need to be designed to limit the volume of unsecured overdrafts, as in real time gross settlement systems, to prevent spillovers across the payments system from the failure of a bank. The availability of efficient money and capital markets is important to allow banks to manage their liquidity, raise

capital, and issue debt. Such markets are best designed with appropriate settlements systems and collateral practices to limit contagion risk. Efficient banking also requires a "credit culture"—an environment in which credit contracts are customarily honored and enforced, in the context of a legal and judicial system that facilitates the enforcement of financial contracts, loan recovery, realization of collateral, and bankruptcy. In some countries, serious weaknesses in the judicial systems can negate improvements in corporate governance and official oversight.

Fostering National and International Supervisory Coordination

The various sectors of the financial system are prone to interact with the banking system in a number of ways, and disturbances in one sector easily spill over into the banking system. In many countries, banks and other parts of the financial system (at times organized as financial groups or conglomerates) are typically regulated and supervised by different national authorities. It is therefore important that regulatory and supervisory policies and practices be harmonized and coordinated, as far as possible, in order to reduce the scope for contagion and regulatory arbitrage. The need for consolidated supervision of financial conglomerates has led to the practice in some countries of designating one national supervisory agency as the lead agency to coordinate the work of all supervisory agencies that relate to a particular conglomerate.[28]

Regulatory standards and supervisory practices are also being harmonized internationally.[29] This not only facilitates consolidated supervision and information sharing among supervisors internationally, but also improves efficiency and can bring important additional discipline to national regulatory and supervisory structures. It is increasingly needed in an environment of growing internationalization of banking, which tends to undermine the effectiveness of nationally focused prudential supervision in a variety of ways, including the use of complex corporate structures and offshore derivatives to evade domestic financial restrictions.

The Basle Committee on Banking Supervision has led efforts to improve cross-border banking supervision, starting with the 1975 Basle Concordat on the supervision of banks' foreign establishments. The Concordat divides supervisory responsibilities as fol-

---

[28]This was one of the suggestions included in the recommendations of the Tripartite Group of Bank, Securities, and Insurance Regulators (1995), but it has not been universally accepted so far.

[29]For example, the Basle Committee and IOSCO (1996b) issued a Joint Statement in August 1996 detailing their coordination and cooperation.

lows. For branches of foreign banks, solvency supervision is primarily a matter for the parent authority. For subsidiaries, solvency supervision is a joint responsibility of both host and parent authorities. In both cases, liquidity supervision is primarily the responsibility of the host authority. For joint ventures, solvency as well as liquidity supervision should normally be the responsibility of the authorities of the country of incorporation. However, the key to effective supervision of foreign establishments is close cooperation between the relevant supervisory authorities. In each case, the bank and its affiliated institutions are to be supervised by the home supervisor on a consolidated basis. The Concordat was reinforced in 1992 by the following four "minimum standards": (1) all international banks or banking groups should be supervised by a home country authority that capably performs consolidated supervision; (2) the creation of a cross-border banking establishment should receive the prior consent of both the host and home country supervisory authority; (3) home country supervisors should possess the right to gather information for cross-border banking establishments; and (4) if any one of the foregoing minimum standards is not met to the satisfaction of the host country supervisor, it could impose restrictions and prohibit the operation of the foreign banking establishment. (See Basle Committee on Banking Supervision, 1992.)

IV

Quality of Information, Supervisory Reporting, and Public Disclosure

This chapter first discusses issues relating to the quality of financial data and difficulties in valuing bank assets. It then examines the types of information required by the various users of data describing the financial condition of banks. The adoption of internationally accepted accounting standards,[30] including the principles of accrual and consolidation, would facilitate the production of high-quality data. In addition, detailed rules governing the valuation of bank assets and the treatment of income and expenditure are often desirable. A by-product of good-quality banking data is a more reliable input to the determination of macroeconomic policy, but that subject is beyond the ambit of this paper. However, to the extent possible, coordination with compilers of monetary statistics will help reduce the burden on reporting entities. The focus here will be on the information needs of two types of recipients with an interest in bank soundness, supervisors, and the public.

Quality of Banking Data

Reliable and comprehensive information on banks' financial condition is fundamental to effective corporate management, market discipline, and official oversight, and thus should be a very high priority. If such information is not available, management decisions may not be conducive to sound banking. Managers and owners (especially in cases where ownership is widely dispersed) may not be aware of the true financial condition of the institution or, if they are, they may wish to conceal it; the public may thus be misled and this may prevent market discipline from working. Moreover, lender-of-last-resort assistance may be misdirected in support of banks whose solvency is exaggerated. In addition, the absence of clear and unambiguous data may make it more difficult for supervisors to resist pressure to bend the application of prudential rules and delay corrective action, in the hope that such banks may recover. Supervisors and courts are then liable to become more susceptible to political interference.

Accounting and Valuation Rules

Reliable estimates of the financial condition of a bank require well-designed accounting principles. Such principles encompass the practices of accrual and consolidation. Particular attention needs to be paid to the use of valuation rules, for example, historic cost, market prices, and estimated realizable values.[31] Accounting rules tend to vary from country to country, but most countries require their banks to value their principal assets—investments and loans to businesses, households and the government—in nominal terms (or according to some index); the value of performing assets can therefore be calculated relatively easily. However, once the capacity of the borrower to honor its debt is in doubt, or the loan contract has been breached and the loan has become nonperforming, the value of the asset becomes impaired.

One way to produce a reliable valuation for bank assets would be to make an estimate of their market price. However, reliable market pricing mechanisms exist only in markets that are sufficiently deep, active, and liquid; such markets exist only for certain types of assets and only in a limited number of countries. Even when loans are legally negotiable, they are seldom traded and it is difficult to identify a clear market value. Thus, objective market-based criteria for valuation of bank assets are frequently lacking, regardless of whether or not sound accounting techniques are used.

Consequently, there is always a degree of uncertainty in the valuation of bank assets and that uncertainty increases sharply during periods of economic distress or crisis. Asset valuation problems are often compounded by macroeconomic volatility or shocks, including high inflation or sharp disinflation, and large changes in exchange and interest rates. Valuation of bank loans or investments in equity or debt instruments can be complicated by poor quality, or lack of, financial data on the bank's borrowers, doubts about the viability of their businesses, and the prospects for the sector in which the borrower operates. Banking information tends to deteriorate further when borrowers and bank managements have a mutual interest in

---

[30]Such as those based on the recommendations of the International Accounting Standards Committee.

[31]For an additional discussion, see Lindgren, Garcia, and Saal (1996), Appendix I.

masking the poor quality of loans in order to keep loans current, and thus avoid revealing losses and possibly losing control over their enterprises and the bank, respectively.

Problems with Bank Asset Valuation and Income Recognition[32]

A realistic valuation of assets and the prudent recognition of income and expense are critical factors in evaluating the financial condition and performance of banks. Since most banking assets are loans and advances, the process of assessing the quality of bank credit and its impact on the bank's financial condition is critical. Otherwise balance sheets may not reflect the true financial condition of the bank and the income statements may overstate profits upon which taxes and dividends are paid. Such an overstatement of profit is primarily due to the failure to establish realistic provisions for potential or actual losses, or to suspend interest on nonperforming assets, which is often prompted by managers' or proprietors' desire to enhance the bank's standing and their own income from it. When timely action is not taken to address problem assets, losses accumulate as opportunities to strengthen or collect these assets are lost and marketable collateral may dissipate. The losses may grow rapidly as bankers attempt to carry problem borrowers rather than recognize the losses and sever the relationship. If left unattended, such losses may threaten the solvency of the institution and, if widespread, the banking system as a whole.

Loan Portfolio Review and Classification

The starting point for any systematic assessment of banks' asset quality is a loan portfolio review conducted by the bank. Under normal circumstances, such a review covers all major customer relationships, including off-balance sheet commitments.[33] In addition, the review includes all nonperforming loans, including those where there are concerns about the ability of the borrower to repay, as well as those that are past due. All loans to connected parties are also reviewed. A sample of the remaining portfolio is selected as it is important to check that loans classed as performing are in fact in order. Credit files and collateral documentation are reviewed on a case-by-case basis to permit an assessment of the borrower's repayment prospects, which depend mainly on cash flow and the business asset conversion or turnover. Collateral is normally viewed as a secondary source of repayment.

After a bank's asset portfolio has been reviewed, it is normally graded according to established criteria. A typical grading scheme used in many countries contains four grades of asset quality: standard or current, substandard, doubtful, and loss. The first category includes assets that are not considered problems. Assets falling into the latter three categories possess various degrees of well-defined credit weaknesses and are typically referred to as *classified* assets. In some countries, the criteria for classification are left to the judgment of individual banks, subject to an overall assessment by the supervisor. However, owing to the weakness of the assessment process in many countries, the application of various rule-based criteria by the supervisory authorities themselves has been found useful. The evaluation of certain classes of high-volume smaller loans such as mortgages, installment loans, credit card receivables, and hire purchase agreements may be based strictly on performance rules derived from historical experience, which can indicate the proportion of substandard assets that are likely to deteriorate into loss.

In the case of large borrowers, sound policy dictates that if a loan of such a borrower is classified in a bank, all other loans of the borrower in that bank should be similarly classified. This could be extended by the supervisor to apply to all other credits to that borrower from all other banks in the system, possibly through the presence of a central risk bureau.

Treatment of Collateral

Credit decisions need to be based primarily on a detailed analysis of a borrower's ability to repay. In the absence of reliable financial information on customers, bankers in many countries typically rely on the collateral provided by the borrower. Overreliance on collateral is problematic because the collateral is often illiquid, difficult to value during periods of financial distress, and costly (in terms of both time and money) to realize through foreclosure or other legal means. While collateral is a valuable protection against loss, it does not replace a careful assessment of the borrower's ability to repay. Collateral and other guarantees need to be appraised periodically, taking into account the financial position of the guarantor, legal documentation, and other factors.

Loan Loss Provisioning

Asset classification[34] of the type described above, together with a general reserve for the remainder of the portfolio (where specific risks have not been iden-

---

[32]This and subsequent sections draw heavily on Bank Supervision Guideline No. 6 in World Bank (1992).

[33]Valuation of some types of contingent financial instruments may be difficult since they are often subject to complex pricing mechanisms.

[34]The process of asset classification is designed to encourage timely action by a bank's management to strengthen or collect its problem assets.

tified), provides a basis for determining an adequate level of reserves for possible loan losses. But other factors must also be considered, including the quality of banks' credit procedures, prior loss experience, loan growth, the quality and depth of management in the lending area, loan collection and recovery practices, and general trends in the economy.[35] There is considerable merit in estimating loss potential on a case-by-case basis, particularly for large borrowers, using provisioning rates based on observed loan loss experiences modified by judgmental estimates.[36]

Tax authorities normally accept that provisioning is a method for recognizing the loss in the value of a bank's assets. Specific provisions constitute a normal operating expense for a bank and should be fully deductible from income for tax purposes, provided that banks consistently apply justifiable loan classification and provisioning rules. Not applying tax deductibility of provisions representing accrued losses amounts to taxation of a loss and therefore, by reducing after-tax retained earnings, would contribute to the decapitalization of a bank. However, when a bank chooses to apply an excessive provisioning percentage, it is not inappropriate for the tax authorities to decline to accept the higher provision as a charge against taxable income (see Alexander et al., 1997, Chapter IV).

Interest Suspension

Another important aspect in evaluating asset quality is a bank's policy on the treatment of interest on problem assets. Inappropriate income recognition policies can rapidly distort banks' financial statements, especially when nominal interest rates are high. Failure to pay interest, or even a delay in doing so, can seriously affect the value of the loan to the bank. Under accrual accounting, interest on performing assets is included in income for the period during which it is earned. However, it would be inappropriate to count as income uncollected interest on loans that are seriously delinquent or where repayment of loan principal is in serious doubt, since the interest is not likely to be received. Where uncollected interest on nonperforming assets is included in income, the bank's profits will be overstated. The problem is compounded in cases where a bank is incurring economic losses but its management is not only reporting inflated accounting profits but also paying taxes and dividends based on those fictitious profits (to conceal the bank's true condition), thus causing a progressive decapitalization of the bank.

It is standard practice in such cases to suspend the accrual of interest to avoid overstatement of bank income and assets. When loans are classified, any future recognition of interest income will only occur as and when interest is actually received in cash. Any interest that has previously been capitalized by an increase in the claim on a borrower, but not received, is regarded as doubtful and is provided for, initially by a charge against current period income. Any previously accrued income that has not been received or capitalized is reversed out of income to ensure that net income for the current period is not overstated. However, a bank needs to continue to record the interest indebtedness of the borrower to substantiate the total level of its claim in the event of liquidation of the borrower or in the event that improved circumstances of the borrower permit full or partial recovery. For this reason, bank accounting systems may continue to record interest due but not received on nonaccrual loans in one account, with a counterpart entry going to an offsetting *interest suspense* account. These accounts enable banks to track, and where required disclose, interest income forgone, as well as to avoid overstatement of assets. In the absence of such accounting controls, supervisory monitoring can be difficult. Bank managers would have increased scope to roll over loans. A typical approach is to require the suspension of interest on those assets that are, say, 90 days or more in arrears or are classified as "doubtful" or "loss."[37]

Implementation Issues

Because valuations of bank assets are prone to manipulation, especially when banks are in financial difficulties, most countries have introduced prudential rules for the classification of impaired assets and provisioning percentages on the lines described above. By applying consistent definitions, criteria, and practices, owners, market agents, and supervisors alike can then analyze the financial condition of a bank. Needless to say, individual loan analysis may still be needed, especially for large credits.

It should be stressed that loan classification and provisioning are principally the responsibility of bank management, which must have in place appropriate accounting, reporting, and control procedures for the appropriate monitoring and classification of all loans and collateral and the follow-up of problem loans. Where minimum requirements for loan classification and provisioning are mandated by regulation, internal and external auditors verify that procedures are in place for compliance and, if necessary, can call for additional provisioning.

Banks' loan loss provisioning and income recognition can be tested and reconfirmed by banking super-

---

[35]When observed loan loss experiences in a country deviate from those underlying suggested percentages from developed countries, such as the United States, required loss reserves may need to be appropriately adjusted.

[36]For additional information on loan loss accounting and provisioning in 14 OECD countries, and other more sophisticated approaches, see Beattie et al. (1995).

[37]For details, see Guideline No. 6 of World Bank (1992).

visors. An essential element in any system is the ability of the supervisors to overrule any provisioning made by banks. As discussed in Chapter VII, this requires that supervisors have the professional capacity to conduct such assessments and have the legal power and institutional authority to call for additional provisions or reversal of income. Such action by supervisors could, of course, force a bank to disclose losses or even admit insolvency.

International Aspects

For international accounting standards to result in transparency of banking operations internationally, some standardization of loan loss provisioning and interest suspension rules is desirable. This is, however, an extraordinarily complicated area in which the international supervisory community, and even the European Union, has failed to agree on common rules or guidelines for years. One regional group of banking supervisors, the Association of Banking Supervisory Organizations in Latin America and the Caribbean, agreed on a minimum set of such guidelines in 1991 (see CEMLA, 1992), but these guidelines have not won wide acceptance in individual countries because of their lack of specificity and the absence of widespread international consensus. The development of internationally accepted rules in these areas, possibly drawing on the World Bank's experience (see, e.g., World Bank, 1992), could make a valuable contribution to strengthening the quality of banking data globally. This, in turn, would directly affect the quality of monetary and other macroeconomic statistics.

Information for Supervisors

The key ingredient in effective bank supervision is accurate and timely information about the financial status and operations of banks within their jurisdiction. This section discusses the types of information a bank supervisor might be expected to request and how they are best measured and collected. Not all countries will be able to meet all of these requirements, at least in the early stages, but they indicate what supervisors need if they are to assess the risks facing the banking systems they supervise. Moreover, in some cases the burden of providing information on relatively low-risk activities may outweigh the benefit to the supervisor and distract valuable management time. But the supervisor needs at least to know where the significant risks are and to have adequate information about them.

Bank supervisors should request information that enables them to (1) assess the decision-making structures and competence of bank management; (2) assess the risks undertaken by the bank; (3) assess current and future profitability and earnings; (4) determine the adequacy of capital and (5) monitor banks' liquidity.[38]

Information to Evaluate Decision-Making Structures and Management

While the effects of concentration of ownership of banks on the stability of banking systems are not well established, detailed information on ownership structure, including any cross holdings in related institutions, helps the supervisory authority discern whether the bank is maintaining an arm's-length relationship with its owners.[39] An excessively close relationship has often weakened incentives for sound credit policies. In addition, if the bank is affiliated with other organizations, for example, within a holding company or conglomerate structure, these affiliations are then transparent to the bank supervisor. Information is also provided on the foreign operations of domestically licensed banks and the local operations of foreign-owned or controlled banks.[40]

One of the most important duties of bank supervisors is to obtain information about banks' management, directors, and major shareholders to assess whether they are "fit and proper" to carry out their respective functions,[41] to help redress the asymmetry of information in these areas between the bank and other market participants. The "fit and proper" test generally requires information about the identity, professional qualifications and experience, competence, honesty and integrity, and personal financial status of the individuals. Such information must be verified by law enforcement agencies, court records, credit agencies, interviews with previous business associates, et cetera. Information detailing business or personal relationships among directors, large shareholders, and counterparties of the bank is also collected to ensure both their suitability and that any financial services provided to them or related counterparties are on a purely commercial basis.

---

[38] This is the basis of the framework known as the CAMELS rating system, developed in the United States, and used in more or less modified form by supervisors worldwide. CAMELS refers to the evaluation of Capital, Assets, Management, Earnings, Liquidity, and Sensitivity to market risk.

[39] For example, the European Union's 1989 "Directive on coordination of laws, regulations and administrative provisions related to the taking up and pursuit of the business of credit institutions and amending Directive 77/780/EEC" requires that information about large shareholders be collected on shareholders who hold 10 percent or more of capital or voting rights or who can exert comparable influence over the management.

[40] Cross-border supervision issues are discussed in more detail in Chapter VIII.

[41] For more details see Chapter VI. The "fit and proper" test is normally a licensing requirement but is also applied on a continuing basis—hence the need for supervisors to keep this information up to date.

Supervisors need to ensure that there is adequate documentation of the bank's decision-making structures, business strategy, and operations. This generally includes the terms of reference of senior managers, their relation to each other, and their respective authorities to commit the bank. Policies and procedures covering the decision-making processes need to be in writing and provided to the supervisory authority.

Well-managed banks also maintain a fully documented business strategy and operations policy manuals, detailing the business objectives and procedures. Such documents are used by the internal and external auditors as well as the supervisory authority to measure compliance with the bank's own strategies and procedures. The supervisor should also have access to full information about the internal control and internal audit systems, and all written audit reports, as well as all reports of the external auditors, including those provided to management but not to shareholders.[42]

The supervisor generally also seeks to ensure that the bank maintains an adequate management information system, which permits accurate assessment and management of the risk position of the bank and accounts for all its claims and obligations. The reporting and recording should be consistent across various types of transactions, and consistent accounting rules should be used for similar types of financial transactions.

Information to Evaluate Risks

The analysis of a bank's risk profile should include both on- and off-balance sheet items and their sensitivities to future events. Quantitative data for this analysis are usually submitted to the supervisory authority quarterly, but information on key areas where changes in risk exposure can take place rapidly, such as foreign exchange positions or interbank funding, may be required on a more frequent basis.[43] On the other hand, most qualitative information is obtained annually or when there is a material change in its content. But it is important that bank supervisors be able at any time to obtain information that they consider important for their risk assessment of the bank. With the increase in various types of risk management techniques, it is becoming increasingly important that supervisors understand the general risk management environment of a bank and not depend exclusively on numerical ratios.

Supervisors place high priority on accurate and timely information on the asset portfolio, paying particular attention to the procedures for valuing assets, classifying nonperforming loans, and provisioning. For most banks, credit risk is the most important risk, requiring the most careful analysis. Here, the supervisory

authority's primary role is to ensure that banks are properly and adequately assessing *their own* credit exposures. Evaluating credit risk requires an understanding of the entire credit process. Hence, an essential element is the written internal credit policy manual describing credit conditions, authorization limits, credit diversification policies, procedures for approval, resolution of problem credits, and credit administration.

Besides loans, other forms of credit exposure are becoming more common. For example, many banks have significant off-balance sheet commitments arising from such items as guarantees and other contingent lending agreements, where there is no claim currently on the balance sheet but where the bank is committed to lend if certain circumstances materialize; very often the bank does so only when the borrower's ability to repay has diminished. These types of commitments are particularly susceptible to poor record-keeping practices, as indeed are derivative contracts. Prudential reports need to indicate the likelihood of conversion into actual credit risk, as well as their collateralization. The credit risk in over-the-counter derivative contracts such as interest rate and foreign exchange swaps can be measured by the cost of replacing the contract should the counterparty fail.[44] In addition, other risks need to be reported, such as the risk in the settlement of some foreign exchange operations that, due to time-zone differences, the bank will pay out in one currency while the counterparty may default before payment to the bank is made.[45] Thus, an analysis of a bank's overall credit risk exposure will typically extend well beyond the repayment risk inherent in the loan book, and will require increasingly sophisticated data-processing techniques and systems.

Supervisors pay particular attention to risk concentration, connected lending, and directed lending as these are the areas where most banking problems originate. An evaluation of risk concentration requires information on the counterparties with the largest exposures, on- and off-balance sheet, and on claims on various economic sectors, industry groups, or geographic areas.[46] Information on loans made to entities related through ownership, family ties, or other links, as well as to large shareholders, nonexecutive direc-

---

[42]The roles of internal controls, internal audits, and external audits are discussed in Chapter VI.

[43]Similarly, monetary data are normally reported at monthly intervals, if not more frequently.

[44]Since credit losses are only incurred by the bank when it is worthwhile for the counterparty to default, only contracts that have positive replacement values to the bank need be recognized as a credit exposure.

[45]The settlement risk associated with differential timing of settlement of the two legs of a foreign currency transaction is called "Herstatt risk," after the 1974 failure of Bankhaus Herstatt, which was closed by its supervisors before delivery of U.S. dollars to counterparties could take place. See also Committee on Payment and Settlement Systems (1996).

[46]To promote international comparability, it is helpful to classify loans by sector and country in accordance with national accounts standards, such as those used in the *System of National Accounts* (IMF, 1993).

tors, and senior management and their families are also reported in detail, specifying loan amounts, terms, and approval procedures. Information on credits granted under government directed lending programs is usually reported separately if they are significant.

Information on loan quality is a key supervisory requirement. The supervisor is typically provided with an analysis of past-due loans by type of borrower, the payment capacity of selected borrowers, collateral, et cetera. As discussed above, this requires that the bank maintain a loan review procedure and a loan classification and provisioning system, incorporating provision for the supervision of interest.[47]

While credit risk remains the most important risk, bank supervisors need to be cognizant of the market risks undertaken by the banks and the sophistication with which these activities are managed, so that they may tailor reporting requirements to ensure that both they and bank management can detect problem situations. The most important types of market risks are specified below. These risks have been separately identified for purposes of discussion, but in practice they are, to some extent at least, interdependent. In fact, one of the features of the value-at-risk (VAR) approach (see Box 1) is that this interdependency is explicitly incorporated.

Virtually every bank operating in an environment of fluctuating interest rates is subject to interest rate risk, which arises as a result of the mismatch (or gap) between its interest-sensitive assets and liabilities. To measure this risk, banks and supervisors need reports on the maturity structure of the interest sensitive assets and liabilities, broken down into several daily, weekly, monthly, or quarterly maturity "buckets." If off–balance sheet items are used to hedge the interest rate gap, a second report showing the position including the hedging instruments is necessary. Furthermore, since interest rate risk can be assumed in currencies other than the domestic currency, reports need to be provided for each currency in which the bank has a substantive position.

Interest rate risk may also affect the value of a bank's portfolio of interest-bearing securities, where these are held in liquid marketable form. The bank supervisor requires information about the types of securities held, as well as a maturity breakdown for each type. Securities in the trading book are always reported at market values, as normally are securities intended to be held to maturity.[48]

A sensitivity analysis showing the gain or loss, by instrument, from a given percentage change in interest rate on the values of interest-sensitive items would also be extremely helpful. More sophisticated reports could show the effects of a change in slope of a yield curve, or other possible interest rate configurations. Regardless of the ability of the bank to perform sophisticated scenario analyses, management should always establish limits on the various instrument exposures incurred by the bank. Supervisors should assure themselves that such limits exist, are reasonable, and are enforced.[49]

Bank supervisors need to obtain information about open positions in foreign currency in order to assess the foreign exchange risk.[50] As noted, a maturity profile of the outstanding exchange rate contracts is also necessary since much foreign exchange risk may be undertaken or hedged through forwards, futures, options, or swap contracts.

Where banks are permitted to hold equity positions in corporate entities whose stock is quoted on major liquid markets, any significant equity risk is reported to the bank supervisor. At a minimum, the report normally provides a measure of total equity risk (the standard deviation in the equity returns over some previous period) or measure of the potential returns due to movements in the overall equity market of which the security is a part. Commodity risks based on changing commodity prices may also be present. If so, a report analyzing the impact of possible changes in value of commodity-based instruments, based on price changes in the underlying commodity, can also be provided to bank supervisors. Equity- and commodity-based risks depend to a considerable extent on the phase of the business cycle and on whether asset prices are at historically high levels.

Derivatives are an increasingly common method of taking or laying off risks, at least by more sophisticated money center banks. It is essential that bank supervisors understand how derivatives can be used for both hedging and position taking and that they collect information on their use by banks.[51] Notional principal, or the principal amount on which various payments associated with the derivative are based, is the most commonly reported attribute of a derivatives

---

[47]Any loan that is not current or deemed to have a distinct possibility of loss is referred to as nonperforming.

[48]The Basle Committee's Core Principles for Effective Banking Supervision do not advocate any particular accounting treatment. In the United States, there is a move toward treating many liquid assets, even if intended to be held to maturity, as valued at market prices as suggested above. Moreover, International Accounting Standard 30 recommends that a bank disclose the market value of dealing securities and marketable investment securities if these values are different from the carrying amounts in the financial statements.

[49]These best practices are drawn from those recently proposed for discussion by the Basle Committee in its *Principles for the Management of Interest Rate Risk* (1997a).

[50]Even when the bank itself has no net position, it may be exposed to risk if it has foreign currency claims on borrowers that do not have foreign currency earnings or if foreign currency assets meant to offset similarly denominated liabilities are in the domestic nontradable sector.

[51]Some countries prohibit banks from using derivatives to speculate, but it is often difficult to distinguish between the risk-enhancing and risk-reducing characteristics of the contracts used in specific circumstances.

Box 1. Market Risk-Measurement Systems

Risk-measurement techniques used by commercial banks have evolved rapidly in many industrial countries, and the Basle Committee on Banking Supervision has agreed that banks, in certain defined circumstances, can use these techniques to calculate regulatory capital charges for market risk. In January 1996, the Committee recommended that national supervisory authorities permit banks to use their internal models for calculating a capital charge, provided that a set of qualitative conditions are met.[1] While the number of banks initially expected to be able to use the internal models option for regulatory market risk capital will be small, a growing number of banks are implementing sophisticated risk-measurement techniques.

Most of the sophisticated models are variants of a value-at-risk (VAR) model, which attempts to measure the amount that would be lost with a specified probability over a predetermined holding period. So, for example, for only 1 percent of the time, for investments held over a 10-day horizon, could the bank expect losses greater than "x" million dollars. When the VAR model covers a number of market risks, the risk-reducing qualities of portfolio diversification can be exploited to reduce capital requirements. Although VAR models may measure market risk more sensitively, they are costly: they are computer-intensive and require large, well-maintained databases of price and position information. The output from such models does, however, depend on the assumptions made and on the validity of the historical data used. A VAR model should not be viewed as a "black box."

In addition to VAR models, banks use stress testing to obtain a richer set of information about the risks in their portfolio of unusual events. A stress test may, for example, assume that some set of interest rates or exchange rates changes by, say, 5 percent and calculate the potential gains or losses on the bank's portfolio. Within a stress-testing environment, the bank can choose the scenarios it views as most likely and obtain quantitative outcomes based on the specifics of their own portfolio. The market risk capital requirements of the Basle Committee recommend that banks have in place a "routine and rigorous" program of stress testing.[2]

The Basle proposals also permit banks the use of so-called Tier III capital. This form of capital, hitherto used by some U.S. securities firms, includes short-term subordinated debt subject to a "lock-in" clause, which provides for it to be converted into equity if the firm falls short of its regulatory capital requirement.

---

[1]Basle Committee on Banking Supervision (1996a), p. 39.

[2]Ibid., p. 40.

---

contract. However, this quantity may be deceptive because it may be hedging other items on– or off–balance sheet. Both positive and negative replacement costs—that is, the actual cost of replacing the contract at current market prices—are better measures of the derivatives position's exposure to market risks. Exposures can be netted against other instruments to the same counterparty where netting is legally enforceable.[52]

The collection of notional principal amounts and replacement costs is no substitute for supervisors' overall understanding of the accounting rules in place in individual banks (as many banks adopt their own rules when there is a void in the traditional accounting treatment), as well as of valuation techniques, effects of leverage, and risk management techniques applied to derivatives.

Because derivatives can be based on many underlying instruments (some financial, some not), their reporting needs to be broken down by the type of underlying market risk as well as the type of derivative instrument, in relatively broad categories, such as those suggested by the Euro-currency Standing Committee for reporting requirements for dealer banks, for example, interest rate, foreign exchange, equity, and commodities-linked contracts.[53] The major derivative instrument classes consist of futures, forwards, swaps, and options. Since options have limited losses when purchased but unlimited potential losses when sold, the risks are particularly great.

Information on a bank's liquidity risk, as well as holdings of so-called liquid assets, typically includes details of the bank's liquidity management methodology, indicating expected future cash flows and the liquidity gaps for specified future periods. An analysis of the liability side will also include information on the distribution, concentration, and types of funding sources, including interbank and central bank sources. On the asset side, banks report information about firm loan commitments, foreign exchange transactions, commitments to purchase securities, and expected shortfalls in cash flow as a result of nonperforming assets. Banks are often encouraged to undertake sensitivity analyses demon-

---

[52]Examples of disclosures meeting these recommendations are presented in Euro-currency Standing Committee (1994), Appendix B, also known as the "Fisher Report."

[53]See Euro-currency Standing Committee (1996)—the "Yoshikuni Report"—Annex 2, for the tabular form of the reporting framework used in the April 1995 survey of derivatives market activity.

strating the effects of changes in their future cash flows.[54]

Some supervisory authorities collect information on a bank's ability to manage operational risk, that is, the risk that business operations, from origination through execution and delivery, will fail to function properly. Such risks arise largely from failures of internal controls, although administrative and technical problems can also be responsible. Some of the most recent published bank problems, such as those of Barings and Daiwa, have been due in part to operational failures. As yet, there are no broadly accepted best practices in this area, but it is clear that the supervisor needs to ensure that the bank has well-documented policies to avoid fraud, including procedures for the taking of disciplinary actions, and that its computer systems are adequately safeguarded against fraud, breakdown, and natural disaster.

Information to Evaluate Profitability

To assess the quantity and quality of earnings and gain insights on the ongoing viability of the bank, income statements provide information on the main sources of income and expenditure, including detailed information on the treatment of loan losses. While supervision is often focused on bank risks, it is equally important to evaluate the strength of banks' profits as this provides the basis for future capital generation, protection against short-term problems, and insight into banks' competitive position within the financial sector. Interest income and expenses are generally the most important categories in the income statement. However, noninterest income from service fees, investments, and trading often augments basic interest income. Details on noninterest income need to be identified, and the volatility of such income assessed. Supervisors also watch for a dependence on volatile or inflation-related sources of income, as this can signal a higher risk profile and potential weakness. Any unusual or nonrecurring income or expenses should also be noted. Information on operating expenses is also important, particularly in relation to a bank's peers.

Information to Assess Capital and Capital Adequacy

One of the most-used indicators of bank soundness is capital. For the purposes of calculating capital adequacy ratios, capital is often divided into several components based on their respective availability to cover losses. Core capital, or shareholders' funds, represents funds that are free and unencumbered by any specific claim by creditors. Secondary, or supplementary, capital may include other items, including subordinated debt. The Basle Committee on Banking Supervision has formulated specific definitions of primary and secondary capital, referred to as Tier I and Tier II capital, for use in its recommended minimum capital adequacy ratio.[55] Supervisors need to ensure that all components of capital are properly defined and accurately and separately reported. When data quality is poor or the condition of the bank is deteriorating, the capital adequacy ratio will typically be a lagging indicator of the bank's condition. Even in good times capital cannot prevent a bank from experiencing problems. But the more capital a bank has, the more scope it will have to deal with its problems.

Information for Public Disclosure

The public disclosure of information about individual banks and the environment in which they operate is one of the most important methods of imposing market discipline. But the value of disclosure depends crucially on the reliability and accuracy of the available information. Without such information, it is difficult or impossible for the stakeholders to appropriately penalize bad management decision making, for instance, by withdrawing funds or selling the bank's securities, or to reward good decision making.[56] In many cases, market discipline can be most effectively exercised in financial markets by other intermediaries. For example, liquidity problems are likely to first become apparent when a bank is seen bidding aggressively for funds from its competitors. Public disclosure of its problems usually follows with a considerable lag.

In principle, the market, depositors, and the general public have no less a need for information than does the regulator. Indeed, some countries such as New Zealand are introducing systems that rely to a much greater extent on the public disclosure of information previously only available to the supervisor. Many others are now requiring greater disclosure in line with the general tendency for transparency in the business of all public companies.[57] For example, the once common practice of banks holding hidden reserves has now largely disappeared. Nonetheless, in practice

---

[54]While the Basle Committee's Core Principles for Effective Bank Supervision do not explicitly require supervisors to collect the specific information recommended here, they state that supervisors should expect banks to manage their assets, liabilities, and off-balance sheet contracts so as to maintain adequate liquidity. See Chapter VI for supervisory recommendations.

[55]See Box 6 for definitions of Tier I and Tier II capital and a discussion of the Basle capital adequacy ratio.

[56]However, for market discipline to operate, market participants need to have sufficient alternative investment opportunities. If the banking sector or nonbank financial service sector is insufficiently large and offers no reasonable alternatives, little reliance can be placed on market reactions to force management changes in banks.

[57]In Norway, for example, information on connected lending is routinely published.

there are in most countries significant differences between the information provided to supervisory authorities and that available to the general public. This is because much of the information provided to the supervisors is market sensitive or contains details about relationships with individual customers, and is provided by the banks on a confidential basis. In addition, supervisors have available much qualitative information arising from bank examinations and regular and informal discussions with bank management.

Public disclosure is generally centered on the publication of quantitative and qualitative information in annual financial reports, supplemented by biannual or quarterly financial statements. However, banks may release other information, such as proxy statements, quarterly earnings and dividend announcements, and press releases on recent or prospective developments. In addition, when banks issue debt or equity instruments, they need to prepare and publish a prospectus that satisfies the needs of potential investors. However, in many countries public disclosure is often "too little, too late," considerably reducing its value.

The information intended for public disclosure should meet the needs of all market participants, including the bank's current and prospective shareholders and bondholders, other banks, depositors, borrowers, other creditors, other counterparties, and the general public. Financial market professionals, who are able to process highly sophisticated information and directly influence or correct bank behavior, may play a useful role in applying market discipline.[58]

Given the sensitivity of banks' liquidity to negative public perception, banks are always reluctant to provide information on poor results. The informational asymmetry between market participants and bank management is thus most acute when information is not positive. Such information, which has the strongest potential to trigger market reactions, is generally disclosed at the last moment, in the least reliable way. When such sensitive information is disclosed involuntarily, the markets' reaction can be very harsh.

Improved disclosure can be brought about directly by law or regulation or indirectly through peer pressure from powerful market parties. In some cases, the supervisor may have direct input into the rules governing public disclosure and, in many cases, there are special accounting principles applied to banks for the purposes of regulatory reporting. It is desirable for the same accounting principles to be used for public disclosure if at all possible. The direct approach involves mandating minimum disclosure requirements, such as requiring banks to publish specified portions of their prudential reports that do not reveal information that could be used by competitors to the banks' disadvantage. On the other hand, in normal times peer pressure might work by showing banks that disclosure is to their advantage in raising funds, for example, if disclosure makes potential investors and depositors more likely to provide capital and deposits.[59]

Market discipline cannot be expected to take over the task of guiding banks' management immediately and fully, but its effect can be enhanced by careful, progressive disclosure once the infrastructure is suitably developed. It is justifiably argued that sudden disclosure of negative information can disproportionately and unnecessarily damage the bank in question or the entire banking system. Thus, any new system of disclosure can best be carefully phased in during a period when banks are sound, and then become a routine matter, thereby reducing the impact of negative information. Moreover, when accounting standards or disclosure methodologies do not yet provide readily accessible information and users are not yet sufficiently sophisticated to interpret the disclosed information, gradual introduction allows time to develop these aspects. This may thus prevent large quantities of sometimes poor-quality information from inundating inexperienced users.

The best practices for information disclosure outlined below contain the minimum information needed for a reasonable assessment of the risks and risk rewards for a bank.[60] Some of the practices suggest additional information to that which is generally available on the basis of statutory requirements. In fact, some argue that banks should disclose all nonproprietary information in their prudential returns. However, of primary importance is the disclosure of information permitting an accurate evaluation of the bank's risk profile, its profitability, and the capital available to support it.

---

[58]This group includes rating agencies who often have access to additional information, in cases where they are permitted direct access to the banks they rate.

Ideally, the information would be tailored to meet the specific needs of the various users, from the least sophisticated depositor to the most sophisticated investor. To satisfy this criterion, there need to be mechanisms that can process the raw information for the benefit of the various user categories. Institutional fund managers, rating agencies, and the financial press perform this function in sophisticated markets, but elsewhere there is often a sizable gap.

[59]In this regard, a mixed approach would be to require that banks issue a specified amount of subordinated debt. Since the price of this debt would implicitly provide the market's assessment of the bank's credit rating, sound banks could benefit by increasing the amount and quality of information they disclose, while unsound banks would be punished if they chose not to do so. However, this approach is only potentially useful if the country has relatively deep and liquid markets for such debt.

[60]The Basle Committee's Core Principles for Effective Banking Supervision do not elaborate the elements of public disclosure, as they are not often technically within the purview of banking supervision. However, as a precondition for effective banking supervision, they state that "effective market discipline depends on an adequate flow of information to market participants" and that such information should be "accurate, meaningful, transparent and timely."

This can fit within the current structure of annual and quarterly financial reporting, with possible additional information provided contingent on certain events, for instance, an increase in reserves, anticipation of large expected losses, or an increase in nonperforming loans.

Generally the centerpiece of public disclosure is the annual report, prepared on a consolidated basis and available to all market participants.[61] The format, typically laid down in statute, contains, in addition to a complete, audited set of financial statements, qualitative information, including for instance a discussion of management issues and the general strategy. It provides the names, other interests, and affiliations of the large shareholders and nonexecutive board members, and information on the corporate structure.[62] It makes clear what parts of the financial statements have been audited and what parts, particularly supplementary disclosures, have not. The financial statements also include information about off–balance sheet items, including some quantitative estimates of exposures to interest rate or exchange rate changes.[63]

Information on the Condition of the Bank[64]

Although financial disclosures of banks are the focus of this section, it is important to recognize that most existing rules for disclosure apply to other financial institutions as well. The European Union's Bank Accounts directive (see European Union Council, 1986), for example, covers other financial institutions and most national laws or rules covering disclosure do so for all publicly traded corporations. Thus, except for the attention to some specific items on a bank's balance sheet, the information needed to assess the risks and profitability of other financial institutions is the same.

The financial statements allow users to discern the general risk profile and risk tolerance of the bank, highlighting the areas in which the bank is taking on exposures, particularly credit risk. To allow a better understanding of the bank's risk tolerance, the report presents quantitative information on the risks and risk provisions, such as the maturity structure for interest-sensitive assets and liabilities, domestic and foreign and currency liquid assets and liabilities, as well as a qualitative discussion of risk-management and risk-control practices.

Banks are normally also required to disclose information on credit risk, including risk concentrations by various broad categories, connected lending, and loans made under directed-lending programs. The user is able to obtain quantitative information on the relation between loans and total assets, nonperforming loans, and loan loss reserves. Definitions for loan categorization, criteria for classifying loans as nonperforming, and criteria for allocating reserves or provisions should be explained. The provision of information on write-downs and recoveries of loan assets is also needed to obtain a full picture of the loan book. Other credit information includes securities and off–balance sheet items broken down by industry type and by credit rating (if rated), including a distinction between domestic and foreign entities. Information on traded instruments (including derivatives) normally includes the gross current losses that would be incurred if counterparties failed.

Disclosure of liquidity risk may be done through the balance sheet and associated notes on maturity structure of assets and liabilities, which enables users to distinguish between the amounts of more stable core deposits and the less stable purchased funds. This information also indicates which assets can be readily liquidated, as well as the level of off–balance sheet lending commitments.

As noted, best practices for disclosing market risks are still being developed. However, the intention is for a bank to report risks from a portfolio perspective whereby all the financial instruments related to the major categories of risk (exchange rate, interest rate, equity, and commodity) are examined together, and financial derivatives should not be looked at in isolation from the rest of the balance sheet.[65] As with credit

---

[61]The accounts of subsidiaries and other affiliates should, ideally, be prepared with the same year end and be audited by the same firm as the parent.

[62]This description, while not represented in the Basle Committee's Core Principles for Effective Banking Supervision, is reproduced in several International Accounting Standards, notably IAS24, Related Party Disclosures; IAS27, Consolidated Financial Statements and Accounting for Investments in Subsidiaries; IAS28, Accounting for Investments in Associates; and IAS31, Financial Reporting of Interests in Joint Ventures.

[63]In the European Union, member states have been required to introduce a harmonized annual accounts format for banks, on the basis of the Council Directive of December 8, 1986, on the annual accounts and consolidated accounts of banks and other financial institutions (European Union Council, 1986). See also IAS30, the accounting standard for banks, and IAS32, dealing with the disclosure and presentation of financial instruments, produced by the International Accounting Standards Committee, which have been adopted in a number of countries.

[64]The recommendations outlined in this section and the next, closely follow those recommended by the International Accounting Standards Committee in IAS30 and IAS32 and those of the Eurocurrency Standing Committee (1994 and 1996).

[65]Recommendations for further improvements in public disclosure for financial derivatives activities can be found in Basle Committee on Banking Supervision (1995b), issued in conjunction with the Technical Committee of IOSCO. These recommendations encourage institutions to utilize the common minimum framework presented in Basle Committee on Banking Supervision (1995a), also issued jointly with the Technical Committee of IOSCO, as this could improve the consistency and comparability of basic annual report disclosures. More recently, the Basle Committee and IOSCO's Technical Committee provided a survey of disclosures about trading and derivatives activities of banks and securities firms (1996b) to follow up the previous survey and update firms about the advances made since the issuance of the November 1995 report.

risk, a discussion of the methods of measurement and the philosophy undertaken in the bank to manage market risk should also be disclosed.

A bank ideally discloses all material areas of market risk. At a minimum, this should include a report on its interest rate–sensitive assets, liabilities, and off-–balance sheet items by maturity. Depending on the risks in the bank's portfolio, the bank would also disclose foreign exchange exposure, broken down by major currency; equity or commodity risks, broken down by major category; and risks associated with its investments or its trading book, at a minimum disclosing the fair value (or market value), the carrying value, if different, and any unrealized profit or loss by security category.

If derivatives (or other instruments) are used for hedging, the bank also needs to explain the hedging techniques that it uses. Regardless of the techniques used, the bank should provide enough qualitative information that the users can interpret the information disclosed. Such a description might specify the types of risks analyzed, the instruments covered and their use within the bank, and a brief description of the methodology.

Information on Earnings

Information on earnings can provide important insights about the longer-term prospects of a bank, enabling the user to determine the main sources of income and expenses and to calculate key indicators, such as earnings per share, return on average assets, and efficiency ratios. A breakdown of total income into interest and noninterest income and a further breakdown of noninterest income may give insights into the "quality" of the bank's sources of income and highlight volatile sources of revenue.

Similarly, expenses are generally broken down into interest expense (permitting users to calculate net interest income) and noninterest expense. To calculate net interest margins, the bank provides the amount of earning assets. Within the noninterest expenses, banks normally report employee compensation, incentives, and benefits, as this is usually the largest category of expense, and any other material categories (for example, operations services, equipment, and occupancy). Specific reserves and provisions also need to be disclosed in the income statement.

V

Public Sector Guarantees

In almost all countries, financial safety nets are considered an integral part of the financial infrastructure and are seen as necessary for promoting the stability of financial systems by enhancing confidence in the banking system. Most financial safety nets have two key elements, namely, a lender of last resort, usually the central bank, and a deposit insurance scheme.[66]

A major problem with any financial safety net is that it undermines market discipline. To counteract this effect insolvent banks must be allowed to fail. Furthermore, the cost of failure should be borne first by the bank's owners/shareholders, at least to the extent of their investment, and then by the bank's larger creditors. Small depositors may be protected under a deposit insurance scheme, where one exists, although in the case of a systemic crisis broader deposit guarantees may be offered. Furthermore, in an effective environment a failed bank's senior officers would be ousted.[67] A gradual phasing out of public sector support would help assist market forces to operate, but would need to be based on the development of the market and be instituted carefully and at an opportune time, as abrupt changes in public policies may have adverse effects. Such changes would need to be accompanied by transparent public explanations of the new policy.

Components of Financial Safety Nets

Lender of Last Resort

Lender-of-last-resort policies typically have three primary objectives: (1) to protect the integrity of the payments system; (2) to avoid runs that spill over from bank to bank and develop into a systemic crisis; and (3) to prevent illiquidity at an individual bank from unnecessarily leading to its insolvency. A central bank may also have a role in ensuring adequate liquidity in financial markets generally, but will also have a responsibility to ensure that its monetary policy objectives are not vitiated by its last-resort lending.[68]

While central banks have a variety of tools that can be employed to achieve these objectives, three are most frequently employed. The first instrument is lending through the discount window to target aid to specific banks. The second and third tools, open market operations and public announcements, respectively, can be used to support the financial system as a whole. The relative importance of these tools varies across countries and according to circumstances, and their use can be influenced by such factors as the monetary policy stance of the central bank,[69] the financial system's institutional structures, and the country's exchange rate arrangements, as well as the degree of market segmentation and widespread weakness in the system.[70]

The very existence of a lender-of-last-resort facility may weaken risk management incentives for banks, causing them to lend more than they otherwise might, and to maintain less liquidity than they would otherwise find appropriate. This tendency can be further exacerbated if lender-of-last-resort support is available at a subsidized rate of interest. The best practices for central banks in normal times were laid out over a century ago, and have changed little since then. (See Box 2.)[71] The key practice is for the central bank to

---

[66]As neither a lender of last resort nor a deposit insurance scheme are under the formal purview of banking supervisors, the Basle Committee's Core Principles for Effective Banking Supervision are silent in these areas. Still, deposit insurance interacts with banking supervision; therefore, some basic principles are discussed in Appendix II of the Core Principles.

[67]If the failure was in part the result of incompetence or inappropriate behavior on the part of particular directors or managers, they may also be disciplined by being disqualified from operating in senior positions in bank management or on a bank board in the future. In addition, incompetent and dishonest managers could be subject to civil suits by bank depositors, creditors, and owners that have suffered loss, or be subject to criminal proceedings.

[68]In some countries, there may be no commitment on the part of the central bank to act as lender of last resort, or lender-of-last-resort facilities may be provided by an entity other than the central bank. Since in most countries the central bank has assumed this role, this section refers to the central bank.

[69]See, for example, Lindgren, Garcia, and Saal (1996).

[70]For example, in 1995 the currency board arrangement in Argentina limited the options available in response to the Mexican crisis. The authorities in some countries committed to fixed exchange rate regimes, therefore, are seeking innovative ways to overcome this problem. One way is to establish sources of external liquidity that can be tapped during crises, for example, through lines of credit granted by international banks.

[71]These were first laid out by Bagehot (1873).

Box 2. Typical Practices for the Lender of Last Resort in Normal Times

- Be available to the whole financial system, but only to solvent, although illiquid, institutions.
- Lend speedily.
- Lend only for the short term.
- Lend only at a penalty rate.
- Lend only if the loan is collateralized.
- Accept collateral at a conservative value in normal times.
- Allow individual institutions to fail and be closed.

---

lend only to solvent institutions and to be prepared to let insolvent institutions fail.

It is frequently difficult to distinguish between illiquidity and insolvency, even in normal periods. This problem can become all the more difficult when there are concerns that denying liquidity support may result in widespread confidence problems that may in turn have the potential to create a systemic crisis.[72] The globalization of banking and finance, the impact that the increased use of derivatives can have on bank liquidity, and growth in international capital flows make the demands on lender-of-last-resort systems more difficult and complex to assess. To alleviate some of these problems, the lender of last resort needs to have access to relevant supervisory information, which necessitates close and continuous contacts with the supervisory authority.

To preserve the incentive structure and to prevent lender-of-last-resort support from becoming long-term funding for the banks or turning into a source of central bank losses, central banks would normally lend short term, with collateral valued at its precrisis price levels, and at a penalty rate. However, even short-term collateralized lending needs to be conservative, since the condition of a failing bank frequently deteriorates rapidly. In such circumstances, continued lender-of-last-resort support may allow an insolvent bank to accumulate further losses. Thus, while the lender of last resort is protected by the collateral it takes, the bank's other uninsured creditors may be made worse off as a result of the central bank's actions.

Central banks are also at times faced with the issue of whether to support just the banking system or the whole financial system. Some countries have adopted a policy of making the discount window available only to depository institutions (which, by their nature, are particularly vulnerable to runs). However, in some cases, the banks receiving central bank assistance are,

in turn, expected and sometimes encouraged to pass on this benefit by acting as lenders of next-to-last resort to their solvent customers. Those that advocate that the lender of last resort rely solely on open market operations, rather than lending to specific institutions through the discount window, argue that liquidity assistance to banks through open market operations will filter through to the whole financial system.[73] However, such filtering may not occur in times of stress when confidence is low and the market becomes segmented. Many central banks therefore combine use of the discount window with open market operations.

In times of systemic crises, the central bank as lender of last resort attempts to assure the public that it will act firmly and limit the scope of any financial disturbance. While there are strong arguments for limiting such support to solvent institutions that need short-term liquidity in a crisis, the need to reassure the public may mean it will be necessary to provide support to banks that turn out to be insolvent. But in many cases, such lending goes beyond the functions of a central bank and therefore needs to be guaranteed explicitly by the government. It is important for a central bank in this position to minimize, for example through offsetting open market operations, the impact on its long-term goals for monetary policy.

In providing emergency liquidity assistance during crisis periods, central banks generally have sought to lend only on a short-term basis, but often without the penalty that they charge for liquidity assistance in normal times, since banks may be weakened due to problems that were not of their own making. When a major part of the banking system is insolvent, it is preferable that a comprehensive bank restructuring plan be designed and implemented, with new capital coming from the government and private sources, not the central bank, and any public costs recognized explicitly (see Alexander et al., 1997). The government may decide that the central bank should provide support until a systemic restructuring strategy is in place, and perhaps thereafter; but such credit would normally be explicitly guaranteed by the government.

Deposit Insurance

It is widely agreed that the primary objective of a system of deposit insurance is to provide a safe asset to small savers[74] while avoiding the moral hazard that market discipline will be weakened. The protection of small depositors, while leaving large creditors at risk, will increase household confidence, help protect the

---

[72]These concerns are generally first raised by the bankers themselves, and they are often able to escalate concerns at the political level.

[73]This argument is made by Goodfriend and King (1988).

[74]Generally, it is not cost-effective to expect the owners of small deposits to monitor the condition of their bank. As noted above, the extent of coverage may vary among countries.

payments system, and thereby provide a measure of stability for the banks. These objectives as well as the basic structure of deposit insurance schemes are conventionally defined in law and regulation.

Protecting deposits may also enable smaller and newly established banks to compete with larger, well-established banks that may be the beneficiaries of an implicit, "too big to fail" guarantee. Thus, it may help to counteract tendencies toward concentration in the banking industry, which in turn may make the banking system more competitive through the possibility of entry by new banks. While some countries have not yet enacted laws or regulations for resolving insolvent banks, the creation of a deposit insurance scheme makes it essential to have such instruments in place. Further, a formal scheme that offers limited coverage can reduce government outlays when political considerations would otherwise compel the authorities to protect all the depositors of failed banks. In most cases, banks meet the cost of the deposit insurance in normal times.

It is desirable that the deposit insurance scheme be sufficiently funded to deal with incidental bank failures and that any disbursal of funds to depositors be executed without delay. Resources may be obtained ex ante by having banks contribute to a fund that accumulates to a target level or by imposing an ex post levy on surviving banks as the need arises. It is also often argued that a deposit insurance scheme should charge a "risk-based" premium that corresponds to the degree of risk taken on by the bank, to ameliorate the adverse selection that accompanies a flat rate premium.[75] When a flat rate is charged, lower-risk, well-managed banks are likely to subsidize the excesses of the higher-risk, poorly managed banks that are more likely to benefit from deposit insurance. However, measuring the risk profile and pricing risk is often difficult. All banks should be members of a deposit insurance system, since otherwise only the weak, high-risk banks will have the incentive to join, negating some of the efficiencies that arise from a broader risk-sharing across banks.

It is rarely possible to ensure that depositors, especially large depositors, retain some incentive to monitor banks and that the banks in turn have incentives to maintain sound practices, unless reliable information about the extent of coverage, procedures governing the use of deposit insurance funds, and the financial viability of the scheme is regularly and publicly disclosed. Some form of co-insurance, whereby the deposit insurance scheme pays only a percentage of the deposit insured or perhaps covers 100 percent of de-

posits to a certain limited threshold, is advisable. Above this limit, leaving some risk with the depositor is also helpful. Since the existence of deposit insurance is often accompanied by some increased incentive to take on riskier activities, it requires strong and professional bank supervision to monitor banks' risk-taking activities.

A system of graduated, calibrated early intervention by the supervisory authority will help to restore problem banks to soundness or allow for their closure at minimal cost to the scheme, and with minimal damage to public confidence. Such a system would enable the deposit insurance scheme to cope with the number of failures that occur in normal times and even with most periods of multiple failures (see Box 3), through a combination of an existing fund and ex post assessments on all remaining banks.[76] However, a workable scheme cannot be expected to handle the costs of a systemic crisis involving pervasive failures. Once a widespread crisis is in progress, the government may deem it necessary to institute a full guarantee, either anew or to override an existing scheme that has limited coverage, despite the moral hazard referred to above. However, it would normally only do so after other options have been rejected and the cost has been fully taken into account, and this only for a limited period.

Exit Policy

Ensuring that banks approaching insolvency leave the market quickly and cleanly is one of the most important aspects of banking supervision policy.[77] An effectively implemented exit policy for weak and insolvent banks that demonstrates that banks will be allowed to fail is essential to counteract the adverse impact on risk-taking incentives created by even well-designed lenders of last resort and deposit insurance schemes. It underscores market discipline by penalizing management, owners, and large creditors. Furthermore, such a policy limits the potential losses that might otherwise accrue to the public sector. While a central bank always needs to be aware of the danger

---

[75]There have been very few attempts to introduce risk-based premiums mainly because such a system forces the authorities to be more open in identifying high-risk banks. Nonetheless, the concept has clear advantages.

[76]Deposit insurance can be made even more resilient, and the costs of the scheme contained further, if the legal system gives the deposit insurance scheme priority over the assets of a failed bank. However, this means placing a greater financial burden on uninsured depositors and other creditors.

[77]The Basle Committee's Core Principles for Effective Banking Supervision acknowledge that prompt and orderly exit of institutions that are no longer able to meet supervisory requirements is a necessary part of an efficient financial system and that supervisors should be responsible for, or assist in, orderly exit. The document discusses neither the potential benefits of rule-based exit policies for countries where the supervisory authority is weak, nor the specific modalities for an exit policy.

Box 3. Typical Practices for a Successful Deposit Insurance Scheme Under Normal Conditions and in Systemic Crises

In normal times, the scheme should
- be explicitly defined in law and regulation;
- resolve failed depository institutions promptly;
- impose limitations on coverage;
- have wide membership;
- pay deposits quickly;
- have adequate sources of funding to avoid insolvency;
- offer risk-adjusted premiums (when risks can be accurately measured);
- have accurate information and disclosure of an insured bank's financial condition;
- grant no decision-making authority for bankers within the deposit insurance scheme;
- take prompt remedial actions; and
- have close relations with the lender of last resort and the supervisor.

In a systemic crisis, a deposit insurance scheme should
- extend coverage temporarily; and
- obtain government backing.

---

that bank closure might trigger systemic problems, the earlier action is taken, the less the impact on the rest of the system is likely to be.

An effective exit policy is not possible without an adequate and effective legal framework and a supervisory authority that has the will, autonomy, and powers to implement a firm policy. In countries where the supervisory authority is still in the process of developing sufficient independence, autonomy and skills, it may be difficult to withstand political pressures to exercise forbearance. In those circumstances, it may be desirable to have rules providing for the use of obligatory graduated corrective measures, ultimately leading to mandatory closure.[78] When capital falls below a certain critical level, there is an incentive for management to try to assume more risk in the hope of benefiting from the higher return; hence, there is frequently a strong likelihood that the bank will, upon closer scrutiny, prove to be insolvent. Early intervention therefore limits the damage to stakeholders in the bank. A rule-based system for intervention in banks can, however, increase the incentives for "window dressing" by bankers, and even bank supervisors, who could be reluctant to intervene if such intervention were to trigger a mandatory response.

Rule-based exit policies can be applied to individual banks. However, in distressed banking systems such a policy would not be viable, as it could lead to a large number of more or less simultaneous bank closures. In these circumstances, care must be taken that the necessary mechanism is in place to manage closures and recovery plans of undercapitalized but viable banks. Such a mechanism could be either inside the supervisory authority or in a separate body.[79] Once the independence, authority, and quality of banking supervision have been enhanced, and the pressure to exercise forbearance has eased, a more discretionary system can be considered.

Conservatorship

When the problems in a bank threaten its viability, the imposition of conservatorship by the supervisory authority needs to be considered. Conservatorship can be described as the assumption of control, by or on behalf of the supervisory authorities, of a bank that is facing serious problems.[80] Under conservatorship it may be necessary to suspend the bank's obligations temporarily, so that time can be gained to assess whether the bank can be put back on track while protecting the interests of the bank's creditors. The conservator establishes the bank's current net worth.[81] If viability seems possible, the conservator may manage the bank until new, qualified shareholders and management can be found. If not, the conservator will initiate liquidation proceedings. Experience in many countries shows that banks placed under conservatorship are rarely restored to profitability without major restructuring and injection of new capital. Ideally, a bank should therefore spend as little time as possible in conservatorship.

It is essential that the supervisory authority take action well before the bank fails. Once a bank starts to experience difficulties in its asset portfolio, its first tendency is to capitalize accrued interest, to underprovision, or to sell remaining good assets, in order to present an artificially high level of capital. During the decline of the bank's condition, the risk of dissipation of assets or looting rises rapidly. Therefore, the decision to impose conservatorship or close the bank needs to have immediate legal effect, notwithstanding possible appeals against such decisions. In the major-

---

[78]In the United States, for instance, the regulator is under a legal obligation to intervene in a bank when capital has fallen below 2 percent of assets. In practice, many supervisory authorities would take some form of action well before that point.

[79]Special arrangements may be required when intervening in and restructuring banks in cases of systemic banking problems, where the closure of many banks is undertaken. These issues are addressed in Alexander et al. (1997).

[80]Different countries use different terminologies. In some, such a person is called a receiver; in others, a temporary administrator. In this paper, the term conservator is used.

[81]Given the high level of business expertise required, the recruitment of suitable conservators may be difficult in developing or transition economies.

ity of cases, banks that have been placed under conservatorship or similar form of supervisory control do in fact prove to be insolvent.

Closing a Bank

Once it is clear that a bank cannot be restored to profitability, or that the use of conservatorship is not feasible owing to either a shortage of qualified persons or a lack of supervisory resources, its license has to be withdrawn, and the liquidation process initiated. The decision that a bank is to be liquidated can result from (1) the supervisor's judgment that the bank is insolvent; (2) the violation of other licensing criteria; (3) missed interest payments or other financial obligations that spur creditors to file a bankruptcy suit; or (4) bank owners' voluntarily desire to close the bank. The first reason for liquidation is the most problematic. The closer a bank approaches insolvency, the stronger will be the incentives to hide information from the supervisory authorities and the markets. This makes it difficult for the supervisor to establish insolvency irrefutably, and makes the timing of the bank closure difficult. The supervisor risks taking corrective action too late, in which case it will be reproached for not taking timely measures, or it risks taking action at a time when the bank will be able to mount a plausible case that closure was unnecessarily imposed and caused material damage to shareholders. While in many countries the decision to liquidate is for the courts, as it affects the interests of creditors and shareholders, it is important that the supervisor have powers to initiate the process and to restrict the bank's business pending the court's decision.

When the bank is insolvent, the loss will need to be allocated among creditors. Most legislative systems have set priorities for the satisfaction of different categories of creditors. Where there is no deposit insurance system, priority settlement to household depositors is sometimes recognized. To ensure problems of moral hazard are kept in check, the primary brunt of the bank's failure needs to be borne by the bank's shareholders. The technical procedure for liquidation is normally laid out in the law, and requires it to be performed by a professional liquidator. This function generally does not belong within the supervisory authority.

Because confidence in a bank can be terminally damaged by a bankruptcy suit brought by creditors, especially if the suit is unjustified, and because there is a need for speedy action, special insolvency procedures for banks are often established. The supervisory authorities may then be able to delay a decision on the bank's bankruptcy, while they investigate whether the bank is solvent or not.[82]

---

[82]In case of voluntary liquidation, when shareholders wish to terminate their business, the supervisory authority should be able to control the liquidation process, in the interests of the bank's depositors and other creditors.

VI

Prudential Regulation of Banking

Banking laws and prudential regulations need to define a framework that induces banks to operate in a safe and prudent manner, and the regulatory and supervisory framework needs to counteract the distortions introduced by public sector guarantees. This requires a consistent set of requirements governing accounting, asset valuation, supervisory reporting and public disclosure, risk-taking and risk management, and entry and exit. This chapter is divided into three parts, covering entry policy, governance and risk management, and quantitative tools of prudential supervision.[83]

Bank Licensing

During the initial establishment of a banking enterprise, it is difficult for potential market participants to distinguish between a potentially successful enterprise and one with a high probability of failure. This problem is due in large part to the asymmetry of information between the new management and owners, on the one hand, and, on the other hand, the potential investors, depositors, and others. Since a bank's viability depends critically on its ability to generate the confidence of depositors and other counterparties, the effects of asymmetric information are most acute during this initial stage. To help bridge this informational gap and create an environment where subsequent market discipline can operate, banks are subject to licensing requirements.

Sound licensing policies are essential, and the licensing process must be both thorough and independent. Because of the links between licensing requirements and the requirements for subsequent ongoing supervision, it is helpful if licensing and banking supervision are conducted by the same agency.[84] The supervisory authority needs to establish whether the prospective banking enterprise will be professionally

managed and financially viable, so that it can filter out applicants that do not meet these criteria. Licensing requirements need to be clearly set out in the banking law, and require a rigorous assessment of management, owners, business plan, and capitalization, which in turn requires knowledge, experience, and judgment on the part of the supervisors. Licensing requirements also need to be objective and transparent to potential applicants and to the public.

The licensing process is designed to ensure that
- the quantity and quality of the initial capital are sufficient (see Box 4);[85]
- shareholders and the management of the bank are "fit and proper";
- the governance structure of the bank, and the structure of any group to which the bank belongs, is transparent and does not hinder effective supervision;
- administrative and internal control systems are adequate;
- the bank has an economic rationale, assessed on the basis of a business plan; and
- in the case of the establishment of a foreign bank, the bank is adequately supervised in its home country (see Chapter VIII).

Banks need to be in compliance with the licensing requirements at all times and the supervisory authority must be able to withdraw a bank's license if any single licensing requirement ceases to be met. Material changes with regard to licensing requirements—for instance, changes in management and ownership or substantial changes in the bank's operations relative to its approved business plan—therefore require the approval of the supervisory authority.

Arrangements are also necessary to deal with financial intermediation that may take place outside the licensed bank sector. This requires powers, whether exercised by the supervisory authorities or not (but on which the supervisors can rely), to deal with the closing down and prosecuting of the perpetrators of illegal

---

[83]Most of the regulatory practices described in this section of the paper have been developed by the Basle Committee.

[84]Although the Basle Committee's Core Principles are silent on whether licensing and supervision should be conducted by the same institution, they do note that where they are different, close cooperation needs to be present and that the supervisory authority should have the legal right to have its views considered by the licensing authority.

[85]The Basle Committee's Core Principles do not discuss minimum initial capital, but do suggest that supervisors should consider requiring higher than minimum capital ratios when it appears appropriate due to the particular risk profile or other characteristics of the bank, and also that no bank should be allowed to operate with ratios below the established minimum.

Box 4. Initial Capital

In most countries, banks are at all times required to maintain a statutory minimum level of capital. Initial capital is intended to finance the initial business of the bank, and to provide the bank with working capital in its early stages of development, say, for a period of at least three years, after which a new bank could normally be expected to be earning profits. Should capital fall below this statutory minimum, the bank would no longer be in compliance with the licensing requirements, and would risk losing its license. In practice, therefore, it is important that banks start with a capital level higher than the absolute minimum, in order to be able to accommodate losses in the initial period of the banks' activities. It is important that shareholders finance the initial capital in cash, on the basis of their own net worth, and not on the basis of borrowed funds. Such an obligation is designed to ensure that the promoters of the bank are seriously committed to its future viability. Experience in many countries has shown that banks are particularly vulnerable in their early years. Indeed, failure rates are much higher for new banks than for old established institutions; capital ratios therefore also need to be higher in a bank's first years.

The level of minimum capital varies between countries. In the European Economic Area, a minimum of 5 million ECU is required. Other countries require considerably more. Banks need to be of a certain minimum size to be viable commercially and organizationally. In exceptional cases, for instance small rural banks established for limited purposes, a minimum of less than US$1 million is sometimes allowed. It is important that statutory minimum capital be made up exclusively of paid-in shareholders' funds.

activity, for example, through the unlicensed use of the word "bank" in business names, or the taking of deposits or otherwise soliciting funds from the public without a banking license. In the case of legitimate financial intermediation outside the banking system, for example, through finance companies not owned by banks, there also need to be arrangements to monitor their activities and, where necessary, to supervise them in such a way as not to promote regulatory arbitrage. Experience has shown that in many countries the activities of nonbank financial institutions can threaten the integrity of the financial sector as a whole.

Management, Nonexecutive Board Members, and Shareholders

Bank corporate structures differ across countries. In most of them, full responsibility resides in a single board, comprising both the day-to-day executive management and the nonexecutive oversight and advisory functions. In others, these functions are divided on the German model between a management board and a supervisory board. Good governance, particularly the appropriate exercise of the relationship between the shareholders and nonexecutive directors on the one hand, and day-to-day management on the other, is the key to safe and sound banking.

Bank managements are required to be fit and proper, that is, they should have integrity, be honest, competent, and technically qualified, and have an appropriate level of banking experience. It is becoming increasingly important for bank management to be highly trained and experienced since, given the growing complexity of the business, less than fully competent employees can cause problems with profound consequences. The track record of individuals applying for bank licenses and the managers they propose should, therefore, be carefully examined. The ultimate criterion is whether the way in which the bank is managed can retain the confidence of the markets and the public.

Supervisors have the power to object to appointments of all board members or members of separate supervisory boards. Since the tasks of nonexecutive board members are primarily to provide strategic advice and to oversee the actions of the management and not the day-to-day decision making, technical expertise carries less weight than for executive management. However, experience and probity should continue to be valued as highly as for management appointments. The supervisor, to the extent possible, investigates nonexecutive board members' other interests and assesses the scope for conflict of interest with the bank's interests and those of its creditors.

The supervisory authority also has a right to object to shareholders, or groups of related shareholders. In case of doubt concerning the shareholders' reputation, or whether they will remain at arm's length from the bank, the supervisor would be able to refuse approval. The underlying criterion for evaluating shareholders is whether they will ensure that the bank is managed as a profitable institution responsible for its financial obligations, rather than for the personal benefit of a selected group of managers or shareholders.

The supervisor therefore needs to be as informed as possible of the ownership of significant proportions of the bank's shares. The transfer or acquisition of significant holdings must be conditional on the supervisor's consent. In addition, the beneficial ownership of significant holdings, and any form of concerted exercise of influence by persons individually holding shares in amounts below the threshold for approval, must be identifiable and subject to supervisory approval. In the absence of supervisory approval, any decisions taken as a result of influence exercised by unauthorized shareholders would be subject to being declared null and void.

When a license is sought by a foreign bank, the supervisory authorities of the home country must give explicit approval. The supervisory authority has a duty to approach the home authority for information on the organizers or shareholders (see Chapter VIII). Additional care needs to be taken when a licensing application is received from foreign individuals who have no connection with a supervised entity and where there is therefore no home authority to provide support.

When banks are part of a larger group of corporations, financial or nonfinancial, domestic or international, the governance of the bank can be influenced by entities that are themselves not subject to banking supervision (see Box 5). This can pose serious risks to the effective exercise of banking supervision. Similar problems can occur when a bank itself is not transparently structured. For example, in some countries bank holding companies often own assets in the real sector as well as banks in other countries, both industrial and developing. In the context of the licensing process, the supervisory authority should not grant a license unless it is clear that the structure of the group does not hinder the exercise of effective banking supervision. For effective supervision, it is important that each regulatory body involved in supervising different corporations within the group establish contact with the other agencies involved and be authorized to exchange information.

Business Plan

A bank requesting a license should be able to demonstrate that it is financially viable by providing a valid business plan setting out its strategy for the first three years. Such a plan would include the results of market analysis, marketing intentions, resources (including staff), expected competition, and expected profitability. The business plan must present the administrative and organizational structure of the bank, including internal controls and the internal audit function, and demonstrate that the projected activities are within the bounds of prudential regulations. In this regard, it is desirable to have an on-site examination of a bank within six months of its opening to ensure that its operations are consistent with the business plan on which basis the license was granted, so that any significant deviations from the plan may be properly accounted for or corrected.

Once a bank has been licensed and starts operations, it will become subject to competition and the discipline of the market and will need to comply with ongoing supervisory requirements. The supervisors and the market will then, of course, need to apply disciplinary measures if the bank is perceived to be operating in an unsafe way. The prudential mechanisms designed to correct poor management and excessive risk-taking are described below. Supervisors will also apply a graduated scale of corrective measures leading up to the closure of the bank if it fails to respond.

Governance of Banks

Inadequate management is an important factor in most bank failures. Banking supervisors therefore seek, as one of their key tasks, to enhance the quality of bank governance.[86] Internal systems and controls, including internal audit functions, as well as persons responsible for these functions, need to be assessed. The corporate structure of the bank needs to be transparent and consistent, striking a balance between promoting safe and sound banking and the flexibility required for effective competition. There should be no uncertainty with regard to management's ultimate responsibility for the bank's actions. The powers granted to the supervisory authority enable it to monitor these areas through the use of on-site inspections and to take remedial action where necessary to protect the interests of depositors. The supervisory authority also needs the power to enforce improvement, including the replacement of top executives, but care always needs to be taken lest the supervisor usurp the role of management.

There must be sufficient checks and balances in the governance structure. Nonexecutive directors and shareholders with voting rights must be in a position to exercise oversight over management and their compensation. Also in this context, sufficiently competent and independent internal and external audit functions play an important role. Contact between the external and internal auditors, nonexecutive directors, and the supervisory authority should permit an exchange of information on the bank's financial condition and management practices.

As discussed above, the supervisors need to ensure that the management meets high standards of competency, experience, and integrity, and that minimum quality standards are met at all times. It must be able to have unsuitable individuals removed. Such removals will normally be subject to appeal, although such procedures should not delay rapid action where that is necessary to improve the bank's management.

The founders and large shareholders of a bank can exercise significant influence over the bank's decision making, and may use that influence to further their private interests. Such pressures can force management to evade normal lending or collection procedures or to extend credit at preferential interest rates and without due credit analysis.[87] Supervisors need to ensure that safeguards against these conflicts of interest are in place.

---

[86]The Basle Committee includes as one of the precepts for its Core Principles that "supervisors should encourage and pursue market discipline by encouraging good corporate governance (through an appropriate structure and set of responsibilities for a bank's board of directors and senior management), and enhancing market transparency and surveillance."

[87]Insider lending is also discussed later in this chapter.

Box 5. Conglomerates

Increasingly, banks form part of so-called financial conglomerates, defined as groups of companies under common control whose exclusive or predominant activities consist of providing significant services in at least two financial sectors (banking, securities, insurance).[1] In many countries, banks can also be part of groups with significant nonfinancial interests. While there are certain economic advantages to such relationships (such as economics of scale and scope), they raise a number of issues that are relevant to effective bank supervision. First, such structures entail the risk of "regulatory arbitrage," that is, the exploitation within the group of differing regulatory arrangements. Second, the bank's governance may be influenced by other corporations in the group that are not subject to banking or other financial supervision. Third, to assess the independent position of the bank, the supervisor needs to be able to obtain information on the structure of the group and on financial flows and relationships within the group, as well as on the financial condition of other group entities. In this context, the question arises to what extent supervision on a consolidated basis is possible, in view of the position of the bank in the structure (parent or subsidiary) and the nature of the other activities of the group. If consolidation is not feasible, the bank

supervisor will need to determine to what extent the risks in the rest of the group could affect the bank.

Special challenges must be faced when a financial conglomerate is active internationally. For effective supervision, full information is needed by each of the regulatory agencies in each of the countries involved, on the group as a whole as well as on its components. In case of problems, supervisory actions will need to be coordinated, internationally and between regulators for the different financial sectors. This can create considerable information coordination and legal problems. To minimize such problems, some countries have found it helpful to designate one national supervisory agency as a coordinator for such groups at the domestic level, and to develop a framework for cooperation between domestic and other international supervisory agencies. Closer coordination of regulatory issues among bank, securities, and insurance regulators on an international basis is currently being discussed by the Joint Forum.[2]

[1]See Tripartite Group of Bank, Securities and Insurance Regulators (1995).

[2]The Joint Forum on Financial Conglomerates was established to bring together representatives of the Basle Committee, the International Organization of Securities Commissions (IOSCO), and the International Association of Insurance Supervisors. Its mandate is to draw up proposals for improving cooperation and the exchange of information among these groups and work toward principles for the future supervision of financial conglomerates.

Money Laundering

The removal of restrictions and controls on capital movements and the globalization of credit, foreign exchange, and securities markets have facilitated the international laundering of the proceeds from illicit activities. Such activities undermine the security and prompt execution of monetary transactions and threaten the efficient and transparent manner in which financial enterprises operate.

Recommendations designed to prevent the use of banks for money laundering have been adopted by the Financial Action Task Force and the Basle Committee.[88] The key elements of the April 1990 Task Force report include provisions that governments should make money laundering a criminal offense. Banks should keep records of their customers' identity, retain records of all transactions for at least five years, and report questionable transactions. Banks should also establish adequate internal control mechanisms and educate their staff to detect and prevent money laundering. Bank staff should be given protection against

liability when reporting suspicious activity. Money laundering should be combated primarily by law enforcement agencies, but supervisors should ensure that banks have adequate preventive systems in place. Also, while the supervisory authority is not always empowered to seek evidence of money laundering, it is often required to inform the law enforcement authorities if it comes across such evidence in the course of its normal operations.

Internal Controls and Internal Audit

The supervisory authority should verify the quality and independence of the internal controls and internal audit function. Processing systems should be checked for reliability and protection against fraud. Sufficient separation should be made between business-generating and accounting functions, particularly in trading areas, where failure to separate front- and back-office functions can lead to significant opportunities for fraud. Credit procedures and approval limits for different management levels should be established. The role of supervisors is to verify that banks have these mechanisms in place.

The internal audit function and adequate systems and control procedures are also key to the preparation

[88]Basle Committee on Banking Supervision (1988b) and Financial Action Task Force (1990). The European Union Council (1991) is also a useful source.

of reliable accounts and the compilation of accurate data. The external auditor generally relies largely on preparatory work done by the internal auditor, and much of the audit consists of checking and verifying the internal audit. The internal audit function is directed toward the effective management of the bank and the appropriate recording of the bank's claims and obligations. The supervisory authority must be able to verify that the internal auditor is sufficiently knowledgeable, and in a position to criticize management when necessary. The supervisory authority also needs to verify that the internal controls are maintained at a level that is appropriate for the types of businesses that the bank undertakes. Internal controls are inspected by the supervisory authorities as part of their routine examination process. To this end, it is important that the internal auditor reports directly to the nonexecutive board members, the external auditor, or, as appropriate, the supervisory authority.

External Audits and Banking Supervision

Like any public company, a bank is statutorily obliged to prepare and publish annual financial statements that are audited by an independent and qualified external auditor (see Chapter IV) and certified that they provide a "true and fair" view of the bank's financial condition. Supervisors may consider requiring that at least one set of prudential returns a year be audited by an external auditor. External auditors of banks need to meet high professional standards. If entry to the auditing profession is well regulated and requires a high level of professionalism, supervisory scrutiny could be limited to the assessment of sufficient experience in, and knowledge of, bank auditing. In some countries, notably in Latin America, banking supervisors maintain registers of acceptable bank auditing firms, while in others the auditor has to be screened annually by the supervisory authority.

The external auditor can be a valuable ally for the supervisory authority, particularly where skills and resources are scarce, and can provide an efficient mechanism for banks to convey to markets that they are providing accurate information and responding to the signals received. In many countries supervisors have traditionally relied heavily on the work of external auditors (see also Pecchioli, 1987), often using them in an on-site inspection function. However, a number of cases over the past years have shown that even highly reputable firms with experienced auditors cannot always accurately assess asset quality. When attempting to verify that the financial statements provide a "true and fair view" of the bank's financial condition, a bank auditor would not normally expect to assess the value of specified assets unless directed to do so. In an increasing number of countries, the external auditor is obliged by law or regulation to inform the supervisory authorities of circumstances encountered in the course of the audit that are relevant to the effective exercise of supervision.[89] This approach has obvious advantages, although ultimately, as the auditor is appointed by the bank and not the supervisory authority, the incentive to act for the supervisors is diminished. When the auditor is under an obligation to inform the supervisor, the auditor should in turn be protected against liability for breach of confidence.

Quantitative Supervisory Tools

Supervisors use a range of quantitative supervisory tools, including various ratios to assess the bank's condition. Such ratios relate to the adequacy of capital, liquidity, large exposures, connected and insider lending, interbank positions, and open foreign exchange positions. However, while such ratios are useful, they are not in themselves sufficient to assess the condition of a bank, and more qualitative appraisals, for instance of management, are essential to obtain a complete assessment. As the financial sector grows in complexity, relatively more attention should be paid to qualitative assessments since rules, particularly those based on quantitative measures, may become easier to circumvent and are more likely to be suboptimal. Furthermore, the accuracy of ratios depends on the accuracy of the data used to compute the ratios, and too much reliance should not be placed upon them if the underlying data are not considered reliable (see the discussion of asset quality in Chapter IV). Sometimes deviant behavior by banks can be detected through peer group analysis and from their behavior over time. Where feasible, compliance with quantitative prudential standards needs to be assessed on a consolidated basis, as well as on a single entity basis, taking into account exposures of branches, subsidiaries, and otherwise related enterprises, domestically and abroad. Experience has shown that without consolidated supervision it is simple for banks to circumvent, for instance, large exposure rules or loan provisioning rules, thus making supervision ineffective.

Capital Adequacy

Banks should have sufficient capital in relation to the volume and riskiness of their business to absorb losses without using depositors' funds. This capital investment gives owners and managers a powerful incentive to run the bank safely and soundly. Traditionally, the adequacy of the amount of capital available to buffer against losses is measured by a so-called capi-

---

[89]See European Union Parliament and Council (1995), the so-called BCCI directive. In other regions, notably in Latin America, banking supervisors have unlimited access to auditors' working papers and are allowed to impose sanctions on auditing firms.

tal adequacy ratio. However, capital is simply the difference between the value of a bank's assets and its liabilities to third parties. Its calculation depends fundamentally, therefore, on the value attributed to its assets (see discussion in Chapter IV on the difficulties in valuing bank assets).

There are two main types of capital adequacy ratios: the "risk assets" method as used in the Basle Capital Accord (see Box 6), and the simpler "gearing" or "leverage" ratio, which is the ratio between shareholders' funds and total assets or liabilities. Both types of ratios tend to address credit risk: the risk of nonrepayment of a credit granted by the bank. Some countries, including the United States, apply both systems in parallel.

The Basle capital standard calls for a ratio between capital and risk-weighted assets of at least 8 percent. This ratio, designed to establish minimum levels of capital for internationally active banks, is now applied in the G-10 countries, as well as in the European Economic Area,[90] and in some 80 other countries worldwide. However, even in the industrialized countries, with relatively well-managed and highly diversified banks operating in an established financial environment, an 8 percent ratio is generally seen as an absolute floor, and the banking systems in most of these countries have ratios that are considerably higher. In developing and transition economies, proper account needs to be taken of the higher risk environment in those countries when determining how the numerator and denominator of the capital adequacy ratio are to be calculated. For instance, the risk weights attached to particular categories of assets could be set at a higher level, to reflect higher risk.[91] For example, if a government has a history of not meeting promptly interest payments on its obligations, the usual zero percent risk weighting may not adequately reflect the risk. Also, the quantitative standard could be set at higher than 8 percent, or the calculation of capital made more limited, thus requiring more capital (see Box 6).[92] This mechanism imposes a natural restraint on the expansion of a bank's risk assets, since more capital will have to be raised to support those assets.

It is sometimes argued that higher capital requirements place banks in such countries at a competitive disadvantage relative to banks operating in G-10 countries. However, the counterargument is that a

---

Box 6. The Basle Capital Accord

The Basle Capital Accord of 1988[1] defined capital, the numerator in the risk asset ratio, as follows: Tier I capital includes issued and paid-up share capital, noncumulative preferred stock, and disclosed reserves from posttax retained earnings. It is the highest quality capital, and should form no less than 50 percent of total regulatory capital. Tier II capital can include a range of other items, including undisclosed reserves that have passed through the profit and loss account; conservatively valued revaluation reserves; revaluation of equities held at historical cost can be included at a discount; general loan loss reserves, up to 1.25 percent of risk-weighted assets; hybrid debt instruments available to support losses without triggering liquidation; and subordinated term debt, up to a maximum of 50 percent of Tier I capital. Goodwill and investments in other banks and financial institutions should normally be deducted. For most banks the use made of Tier II capital is much less than 50 percent.

The bank's assets are divided into four or more categories of risk, for instance, commercial loans, mortgage lending, interbank debt, and government debt. For each risk category, a risk weighting is established. This weighting, or coefficient, is applied to the total amount of assets in each category. Normal credit risks are assigned a 100 percent rating, while the other risk categories carry a lower weighting, based on the risk of that category relative to normal credit risks. The amounts obtained for each of the categories are added to obtain the total of "risk-weighted assets," which is the denominator of the risk-weighted ratio. Off–balance sheet items are also included in the ratio, converted into credit equivalents by applying conversion factors reflecting the degree to which an off–balance sheet items reflect expected on–balance sheet credit commitments of the bank.

The Basle Committee considers that the risk-weighted ratio has three advantages over the gearing ratio. First, it does not penalize banks for holding relatively low-risk assets such as government securities; second, it allows for incorporation of off–balance sheet items; and third, it allows for better international comparisons of banks with different balance sheet structures.

---

[1]Basle Committee on Banking Supervision (1988a).

---

[90]The G-10 countries comprise Belgium, Canada, France, Germany, Italy, Japan, the Netherlands, Sweden, Switzerland, the United Kingdom, and the United States. The European Economic Area comprises the European Union member states, Iceland, Liechtenstein, and Norway.

[91]The Core Principles acknowledge that supervisors should consider requiring higher than minimum capital ratios when it appears appropriate, and stresses that the standard is a minimum requirement.

[92]Also see Dziobek, Frécaut, and Nieto (1995).

higher ratio basically reflects higher risk, for which the bank needs an adequate buffer.

Therefore, the basic issue when a country describes itself as using the "Basle" model is not whether the system is faithfully copied or not, but whether the appropriate adaptations have been made to reflect local conditions. Unless the proper loan provisioning and interest suspension rules have been applied, capital may be overstated to the point where any ratio analysis becomes meaningless (Dziobek, Frécaut, and Nieto, 1995). Moreover, ratio analysis needs to be complemented by a qualitative assessment of the bank's ability to manage its risks.

The traditional capital adequacy ratios were developed to address the credit risks in banks' portfolios. But banks also carry other significant risks for which a capital buffer is required, notably market risk—that is, the risk of a change in the market value of an asset or commitment. This type of risk is inherent in banks' holdings of trading portfolio securities, financial derivatives, and open foreign exchange positions. Banks are also vulnerable to interest rate risk when there is a substantial difference between the effective maturities, or pricing intervals, between liabilities and assets. Capital adequacy standards against such market risks are now being introduced.[93]

Liquidity

A key element of banking supervision is monitoring the liquidity of banks. This task becomes even more critical when a bank starts to encounter problems, and market availability of liquidity may decline for that bank. The interbank deposit market, nationally and internationally, is particularly sensitive to hints of difficulties faced by a bank, sometimes overreacting by rapidly withdrawing funding. Although this is an example of the very direct effect of market discipline, it could force the bank to liquidate assets quickly, moving the market against it, and possibly force the bank into insolvency, even if initially the bank was merely illiquid. In a certain sense, then, market discipline may be very harsh. It can be argued that this can be alleviated to a certain extent for solvent banks, by lender-of-last-resort liquidity support as discussed above, but a bank cannot be sure that a well-designed lender-of-last-resort facility will automatically be available to it (see Chapter V).

There are no internationally agreed prudential standards on bank liquidity, although the Basle Committee has issued material discussing some of the fundamental issues.[94] But supervisory authorities require banks to have adequate internal systems to monitor and control their liquidity needs and establish contingency plans for periods of liquidity stress, resulting either from overall market problems or from institution specific crises. For large internationally active banks,

systems need to be very sophisticated and include simulation models for a variety of scenarios. An overdependence on one or few funding sources should be avoided. Limits are applied by a number of countries on funding from a single source or a connected group of sources.

In many countries, central banks require commercial banks to maintain high reserve requirements in relation to deposits. Although such reserves are intended primarily for monetary purposes, they do serve some prudential purposes as well. Some central banks or prudential authorities also impose liquid asset requirements; such requirements ideally allow banks to select from a range of liquid assets and not become schemes for obligatory holding of government securities. In general, banks need to be encouraged to retain a certain proportion of their assets in liquid and low-risk securities that can generate cash quickly.

Access to central bank liquidity facilities, such as Lombard facilities and discount windows for rediscount of government paper, also forms a part of banks' contingency planning for liquidity emergencies. Such borrowing is costly, and banks need to hold the collateral required for access to such facilities, so banks will typically avoid using it. Central bank facilities may, however, play a relatively important role when local interbank and other money markets are thin or segmented.

Credit Diversification

Well-managed banks limit their exposure, including off–balance sheet items, to a single borrower or related group of borrowers, to diversify risks and avoid the risk that failure of one large borrower or related group of borrowers may lead to excessive losses. The supervisor monitors such credit concentrations and generally prescribes limits. The Basle Committee has called for and the European Union has set a limit of 25 percent of regulatory capital (Basle Committee, 1991) for exposures to single borrowers or related groups of borrowers. The European Union defines an exposure larger than 10 percent of regulatory capital as a large exposure. In the United States, federal regulations set the limit at 15 percent of a bank's regulatory capital for unsecured loans and an additional 10 percent for loans secured by specific and liquid marketable security. The European Union has set the aggregate limit for all large exposures at 800 percent of regulatory capital. Other countries, for example, the United States, have no aggregate limits. Other forms of risk concentration, which are generally not subject to strict ratios, are concentrations in specific economic sectors—for example, the real estate or agricultural sectors—or geographical concentration. For risk concentration rules to be effective, compliance with them must be assessed on a consolidated basis, taking into account exposures incurred by branches, subsidiaries,

---

[93]See Basle Committee (1996a). This also envisages the use of integrated VAR models and Tier III capital, which is explained briefly in Box 1.

[94]Basle Committee (1997b). The Core Principles recognize the elements of strong liquidity management ("good management information systems, central liquidity control, analysis of net funding requirements under alternative scenarios, diversification of funding sources, and contingency planning") and recommend that banks have a diversified funding base and maintain adequate liquid assets.

or other related enterprises. Gross exposure, not taking account of collateral, is a conservative basis for the application of exposure limits.[95] If deductions are to be made, only very secure collateral, under the direct control of the bank, and valued very conservatively, should be taken into account. Many supervisors set standards for the maximum percentage of the value of collateral that can be taken into account, especially when the values of certain types of collateral are volatile.

The definition of a related group normally takes into account conditions in a given country and may require a degree of judgment. In the European Union, two or more borrowers constitute a single risk if one of them directly or indirectly controls the others, or if they are so closely related that if one were to experience financial problems the others would be likely to encounter repayment difficulties. Indications of such relationships include common directors, cross guarantees, or common ownership.[96] In a number of cases, the supervisors will need to exercise judgment. The use of consolidated accounts is, in itself, not a sufficient criterion as exposure by unconsolidated companies owned by the same owner should also be seen as related.[97]

Connected Lending

Loans to counterparties connected to the bank, for example, directors, managers, shareholders, and their families, have contributed to banking problems in many cases; large loans to such borrowers, or to companies owned by them, can easily become uncollectible and cause losses. In view of the increased risk resulting from the conflict of interest between the bank and the borrower, many supervisors reserve the right to deduct such loans from capital, when, in the judgment of the supervisor, the loan was not made on an arm's-length basis. Connected lending represents an obvious breakdown of market discipline and poses considerable risk to the bank. Such loans are normally required to be disclosed and they may need the intervention of the supervisor.

Foreign Exchange Exposure

Well-managed banks should possess a system of internal limits and monitoring mechanisms for their open positions in specific currencies, including sub-limits on spot positions and various forward maturities when derivative instruments are used, as well as an overall limit for the net open position.[98] Uncovered open positions in foreign exchange have been an important factor in many banking problems. Since position data are considered to be proprietary and are thus not usually available to other market practitioners, such open positions are closely monitored by supervisors and often subject to limits, which are related to exchange rate volatility.

Several methods are used to measure aggregate positions.[99] The appropriate summary measure of an open position depends on the correlation among exchange rate changes between the currencies in which a bank holds open positions. If exchange rate movements are perfectly correlated, the net aggregate position is appropriate, while if movements are completely uncorrelated, then the gross aggregate position is in order. The shorthand aggregate position is a compromise between the other two measures, and has been recommended by the Basle Committee and the European Union.[100] On the other hand, some countries intend to include foreign exchange positions in an overall approach to market risk capital adequacy and allow banks with adequate management and control systems on their dealing operations to hold foreign exchange and other proprietary market positions limited only by the availability of capital to support them.[101]

Limits on Nonbank Activity

The objective of limits imposed on banks' equity holdings in nonfinancial enterprises is to prevent banks from using depositors' money to take risks outside the scope of traditional banking, and to limit conflicts of interest and concentrations of financial power. Excessive diversity of activities and equity interests could also create difficulties in consolidating accounts

---

[95]The existence of risk-based capital requirements places an implicit limit on credit exposures since, to take on more credit risk, additional capital will need to be raised. At some point, the cost of raising additional capital becomes prohibitive, relative to the benefits, thereby limiting extensions of credit. However, concentrations within the general risk categories (e.g., to a connected group) will not be adequately accounted for within this framework and may require explicit limits.

[96]See European Union Council (1992b), Article 1m.

[97]In the United States, consolidation depends on a series of tests, including such factors as whether the loans have a common repayment source, common control, or financial independence, or are being used for a common end.

[98]The Core Principles for Effective Banking Supervision recommend that banking supervisors ensure that bank management has set appropriate limits and implemented adequate internal controls for their foreign exchange business.

[99] For example, the definitions typically used are: "gross aggregate position," which is the sum of all open positions in foreign currency, short or long; "net aggregate position," which is the difference between the sum of all long positions and all short positions; and the "shorthand method," adopted by the Basle Committee and European Union, which separately sums all short positions and all long positions, with the larger of the two totals to be regarded as the overall open position.

[100]Basle Committee (1996a), p. 23. The report also discusses the use of a bank's own VAR model (see Box 1), which can fully take account of correlations between currencies.

[101]Also see Hartmann (1995), and Basle Committee (1996a).

and exercising supervision. Banks' business is therefore often limited to well-defined financial activities, where managements have the necessary expertise. Also, within the supervisory authority, expertise is required in those areas in which the bank is conducting business. If expertise is limited, limiting the banks' activities ensures that the bank does not take risks that cannot be supervised.[102]

---

[102]The Core Principles do not explicitly advise supervisors to limit nonbank activities but do advocate that the scope of activities governed by banking licenses be clearly defined and that supervisors must be satisfied that banks have in place a comprehensive risk management process to identify, measure, monitor, and control all material risks.

The scope of permissible financial activities differs across countries. A broad distinction can be made between banking systems where banks are permitted to engage in securities business and those where they are not. In the European Union, banks are permitted to engage in securities business under their own name or by means of a subsidiary, and they are frequently in common ownership with insurance companies. In some countries, banks also have substantial interests in industrial companies. In other countries, such as the United States and Japan, banks are more narrowly confined and are permitted to engage in securities business only to a limited extent. In all cases, the supervisory authorities should be aware of banks' equity holdings and be able to force the bank to divest when necessary.

VII

Supervisory Oversight

This chapter examines the attributes of an effective banking supervisory system. It is based on practice established in major supervisory authorities, and to a large extent reflected (sometimes only implicitly) in the published recommendations of the Basle Committee.[103] The first issue addressed is the degree of supervisory autonomy, which is necessary to permit the supervisory authority to perform its responsibilities without undue political interference and to allow the authority to acquire and allocate its financial and staff resources. The second issue relates to the tools that should be provided to the supervisory authority to carry out its mandate. The third section of this chapter addresses the powers of the supervisory authority to request information from and cooperate with other financial sector supervisors and law enforcement agencies. The fourth issue pertains to the choice of location for the banking supervisory function within the public sector. The fifth section discusses the characteristics of off-site analysis and on-site supervision. Finally, this chapter discusses the appropriate range of remedial and punitive measures available to the supervisory authority.

Autonomy of Banking Supervision

To allow the supervisory authority to resist undue pressures from banks themselves, their shareholders, depositors and other creditors, borrowers, or the government, the objectives and purposes of the supervisory authority and its autonomy should be as firmly spelled out and entrenched as possible by law. It is also in the interest of the banking sector to have certainty regarding the scope of authority of the supervisory authority.[104]

The law detailing the authority of the supervisor normally contains the following objectives: (1) to protect the supervisory agency against undue political influence in the exercise of its mandate, specifically concerning decisions with regard to individual banks, licensing, vetting of large shareholders and managers, compliance and withdrawal of licenses, and closure and liquidation; (2) to provide authority for the issuance of prudential regulations and standards and to protect the supervisory agency against undue outside influence regarding the issuance of such regulations and their content and other regulations issued in the interest of the proper exercise of banking supervision; (3) to protect the agency against undue influence in the implementation of its loan classification and provisioning rules, monitoring, and inspection tasks; (4) to protect proprietary information of the commercial banks and of the supervisory agency itself against unwarranted disclosure; (5) to protect staff of the supervisory agency against personal liability for decisions taken in the exercise of their duty; (6) to ensure financial autonomy of the supervisory agency; (7) to ensure the autonomy of the agency in its internal organization and procedures; and (8) to create an appropriate system to ensure the accountability of the supervisory authority.

Political Autonomy

To be effective, a supervisor needs sufficient political autonomy to take necessary measures. There are many examples in which supervisors have been persuaded to exercise forbearance and to believe that with a delay the bank could work its way back to being financially sound. However, a near-insolvent bank faces strong incentives to assume additional risks, and hence forbearance has rarely been a successful solution.[105]

While there is no way of legally constructing a supervisory regime that will entirely eradicate the possibility of undue influence being exerted, there are a number of areas where appropriate policies may re-

---

[103]See the various papers now published in Basle Committee (1997b).

[104]The Core Principles for Effective Banking Supervision support a system of banking supervision whereby clear responsibilities and objectives are delineated and operational independence and adequate resources are maintained. The objectives are similar to those suggested above, although the Basle Committee explicitly refers to the possibility of multiple supervisors, whereas a single authority is envisioned here.

[105]Countries with an effective supervisory authority have sometimes found limited forbearance useful when banks are viable business institutions, although technically insolvent.

duce the risk of such influence being applied. Among these are the legal status and powers of the supervisory agency; the location of the supervisory function; the dichotomy between rules and discretion; the need for transparency, an appeal and judicial review process, market discipline, and professional competence; and a fixed term of tenure for the head of the banking supervisory authority, appointed by the legislative body.[106]

Appropriate supervisory policies and procedures can be identified on a rules versus discretion continuum. A system heavily dependent on compliance with transparent rules and regulations lies at one end of the spectrum, while a system that gives the supervisor objectives but leaves the agency free to use whatever powers it thinks fit to achieve its goals lies at the other. The justification for discretion is that bank supervision is as much about making qualitative judgments about the integrity and competence of management as it is about maintaining compliance with quantitative rules or prudential ratios. However, one major problem with allowing supervisors discretion is that there is no guarantee it will be used impartially and objectively. Much depends on the integrity, public credibility, and competence of the supervisor, which can only be earned over time, as well as on the broader political and institutional environment.

An effective banking supervisory system therefore needs to be sufficiently transparent that the supervisors can be seen to be exercising their powers in a way that is beneficial to the objectives of maintaining a stable and sound banking system. One way of achieving such transparency is to provide for periodic reports to be published describing the actions that have been taken by the supervisory authority to achieve its objectives. In this way the supervisor's performance can be monitored by government, by the supervised banks, and by the public at large. Of course, there may well be justifiable reasons why the supervisor's actions in specific cases can only be revealed some time after the event, but the knowledge that they will ultimately have to be revealed can be a powerful tool.

The institution of a system in which banks, as well as individual shareholders, directors, and managers can within the limits of the law appeal against the actions of the supervisor is a useful element in ensuring the accountability of supervisors. It thus helps justify giving the supervisor discretion. It also reinforces the supervisor's autonomy from undue political influence.

A supervisory process based on best market practice is likely to retain more support from the banking sec-

tor. This may give the supervisor more influence in resisting pressures that derive from special interest groups. A supervisory body that can demonstrate a high degree of professional competence may find it easier to earn a position vis-à-vis the interested parties that enables it to resist improper pressure more readily.

Staffing and Resources

Without sufficiently qualified staff, the supervisory authority cannot fulfill its mandate. The banking supervisory authority needs to develop an on-site bank examination capacity with investigative resources and an off-site analytical capability, as well as being open to market intelligence and possessing an awareness of macro-prudential developments. Supervisors need examiners with knowledge and skills of the business of banking to be able to assess management adequately, including the control systems they employ. They need sufficient familiarity with banks' operations to know where to look and probe for weaknesses that may not be evident on the surface. Banking supervision staff need to have the ability to evaluate credit approval and monitoring systems and to assess the payment capacity of debtors, adequacy of provisions, et cetera. Increasingly, inspectors need the skills required to assess the efficacy of sophisticated risk management systems and the adequacy and vulnerability of electronic data processing systems used by banks. Off-site analysts need to be able to absorb and assess such information and direct examiners to areas of weakness. Skills to detect inconsistencies and identify potentially damaging trends are also important. In addition, when the supervisor suspects fraud or other illegal activity that may threaten the soundness of individual banks, he or she needs the capacity to investigate quickly and in depth. The banking supervisory authority also needs to develop effective working contacts with other supervisory bodies both at home and abroad.

The banks can contribute substantially to the work of supervision. For example, banks can complete their own calculations of required prudential ratios. Much of the work going into an examination can be facilitated by the banks, particularly by the internal audit function and external auditors.[107] The supervisory authority may also contract external computing and information systems specialists, lawyers, forensic accountants, former commercial bankers, or others with special skills, to conduct specialized tasks.

To be able to attract and retain qualified staff, a supervisory agency needs flexible pay and personnel policies that will enable it to recruit at appropriate levels people with the requisite skills. In many countries,

---

[106]A fixed term can also have disadvantages. The power of the supervisor can, for instance, be weakened when the term of office is close to expiration. If the term is renewable, the supervisor may be subject to pressure in order to secure a renewal. On balance, however, the advantages of a clear mandate for a fixed term period seem to outweigh any disadvantages.

---

[107]See Chapter VI for more details on the interactions between supervisors and internal and external auditors.

excessive differentials between pay levels for bank inspectors and commercial bankers lead to excessively rapid turnover of qualified staff and conflicts of interest. It is essential that banking supervisory staff be seen to be free from conflict of interest, from financial connections to any bank, and from obvious political or business affiliations.

The supervisory authority also needs some financial autonomy. It may have its own sources of income, for instance in the form of direct funding as part of central bank expenses, or indirect assessments upon the banks,[108] or as a direct lump sum budget allocation—or a combination of these—with the freedom to use these funds provided they are used in the proper exercise of its mandate. General oversight of a state accounting office could be considered, as well as an independent external audit.

Immunities

Banking supervision can substantially affect the conduct of business of a bank and the property rights of its owners. Situations can arise in which the bank, its owners, or its managers feel that their interests have been unjustly damaged by the actions of the supervisors. Although it should be possible for interested parties to appeal against any specific decision of the supervisory authorities with regard to an individual bank, the process is more effective if the supervisors themselves are not personally liable for damages caused by any actions legitimately performed in the course of their duties. The supervisory authority as such could conceivably be held liable for damages if it took obviously unreasonable and damaging decisions against the bank or its owners or managers. The criterion of reasonableness should only take into account the circumstances at the time the action was taken; liability need not be so strict that it could unduly hinder taking sufficiently speedy supervisory decisions and actions.

Powers of the Supervisory Authority

Ideally, the supervisory authority is endowed by law with a clear mandate and powers to carry out its function. The law defines the scope of authority of the supervisor and confers authority to license and to withdraw licenses of financial institutions, approve new owners, issue prudential regulations, obtain periodic prudential reports, conduct on-site inspections, take corrective actions (including the imposition of restrictions on banks' business activities), and close and liquidate banks. Actions taken by the supervisor to remedy an unsafe or unsound situation have immediate legal effect, notwithstanding appeals procedures. Which types of financial institutions are subject to supervision differs from country to country. Banks, credit unions, cooperative banks, mutual fund-type institutions, and investment funds are some of the categories of institutions that are included. For the purposes of this paper, the scope of the banking supervisory authorities is, as noted earlier, limited to banks defined as institutions that make it their business to take deposits or other nominally repayable funds from the public, and grant credits and make investments for their own account.[109] For a supervisory system to be effective, such institutions need to obtain a banking license and thereby submit themselves to banking supervision. Unlicensed institutions that perform banking activities can then be prosecuted.[110]

An effective supervisory authority has at least the following powers:

- Exclusive authority to license and to withdraw licenses. For optimal effect, these two functions should be exercised by one and the same agency (see footnote 20).
- Authority to issue prudential regulations and standards. Ideally, detailed requirements are not in the law itself as the parliamentary procedure may be insufficiently flexible to incorporate new or revised standards efficiently and quickly. The broad areas in which the supervisory authority is authorized to issue regulations are, however, normally laid down in law, thus providing an element of stability to the supervisory framework.[111] Preferably the banks are consulted on proposed changes, avoiding, however, the possibility of undue influence or "regulatory capture."
- Authority to obtain periodic reports in the format and periodicity established by the supervisory authority.[112] Banks can be required to show their own assessment of their compliance with the prudential ratios and limits. Untimely, incomplete, or incorrect submittal of the reports is subject to an administrative penalty, and ultimately to prosecution.

---

[108]Direct assessments are normally based on the size of the bank, but can also contain some element of cost-based fees, so that those banks that are onerous to supervise are not subsidized by the well-run bank that costs little to supervise.

[109]The Core Principles for Effective Banking Supervision clearly state that the term "bank" should be reserved for those institutions licensed and supervised as banking institutions.

[110]Also see Article 1 of the European Union Council (1989).

[111]The supervisory authority is normally authorized to issue regulations in at least the following fields: minimum initial capital in the context of bank licensing, capital adequacy, liquidity, risk diversification, market risks such as open foreign exchange positions, securities, interest rate risk, equity investments, loan classification and provisioning, internal control systems, and accounting and reporting. See Chapters IV and VI.

[112]The content of such reports is described in Chapter IV and VI.

- Authority to conduct on-site inspections. These are necessary to verify the information submitted and are also essential to assess management quality. Inspectors have full powers to enter the bank, inspect any information they consider useful, in whatever form, and have access to the management and any staff of the bank. Refusal to permit an inspection or to cooperate with the inspector is subject to an administrative penalty, and ultimately to prosecution. Supervisors also have the right to obtain information from all consolidated subsidiaries or equity holdings of the bank, as well as connected nonconsolidated entities.[113] Staff from nonsupervisory agencies do not participate in the inspection, nor are the results of an inspection shared routinely with them.

- Authority to take corrective actions. In case of breach of prudential regulations or of unsafe and unsound banking activities, the supervisor should be able to impose a progressively severe set of administrative penalties on individual managers of the bank, have them removed from office, or issue "cease and desist" orders constraining the business activities of the bank. Such action, which falls short of conservatorship or closure, can be kept confidential or publicly announced, according to the circumstances.

- Authority to take emergency action. Such actions can consist of the removal of management powers and the imposition of conservatorship. The conservator works under the close supervision of the supervisory authority and reports to it regularly. The conservator could be given the authority to obtain professional assistance, such as legal advice or auditing services.

- Authority to close and initiate the liquidation of banks. In cases of insolvency, gross and repeated breaches of regulations or other extremely unsafe banking practices, in cases of criminal behavior by, or tolerated by, the bank, and in cases of continued noncompliance with the licensing requirements, the supervisory authority has the powers to withdraw the license and close the bank. This includes the power to take control of the assets and to prevent looting of the bank. Liquidation should not normally be performed by the supervisory agency itself.

- Authority over the bankruptcy of banks. In light of the extreme vulnerability of confidence in banks, which could be very seriously damaged by an unfounded bankruptcy suit, a form of control by the supervisory agency over whether bankruptcy proceedings are started against a bank is sometimes considered.

Interaction with Other Financial Sector Supervisors and Law Enforcement Bodies

The increasing linkages between domestic financial sectors and the internationalization of financial services have greatly increased the need for closer cooperation between different financial sector regulators domestically and internationally. The combat of criminal activities involving the financial sector has required closer cooperation with law enforcement agencies as well.

Cooperation between supervisors of different financial sectors is necessary, for instance, when there are corporate linkages between banks, securities, and insurance companies.[114] It may be necessary to obtain information about prospective bank managers that have previously worked in other financial institutions. The exercise of consolidated supervision may require taking measures against the establishment of a bank in another jurisdiction. Cooperation among different financial sector supervisors may be made difficult by different laws applying to banking, insurance, or securities business, for instance in the areas of licensing, prudential regulations, and accounting standards. It may be difficult to produce consolidated accounts of banks and insurance companies, for example. The exchange of information between supervisors can be hindered by confidentiality constraints that apply to each of the different regulators. Barriers of this nature should be removed. Supervisors over different financial sectors should be able to exchange information freely on individual institutions.[115]

It is essential that the supervisory authorities retain the trust of the banks, in order to be truly effective as supervisors and to be able to take proactive measures. Supervisors generally need at their disposal well-documented and easily accessible information about the banks. This makes the supervisory authorities an ideal witness in court cases against banks and their clients. However, if inappropriately used as witnesses, supervisors risk losing the confidence and trust of the banks. Thus, the supervisory authorities may need to be protected against excessive requests by the law enforcement authorities to provide information about banks. They should, however, be prepared to provide information in case of specific suspicions of criminal behavior, money laundering, or tax fraud, and upon an official request from the authorities.

---

[114]For issues related to the regulation and supervision of conglomerates that provide such financial services as banking, securities, investment management, and insurance, see Scott (1994).

[115]The Joint Forum on Financial Conglomerates is currently working to document existing impediments to information exchanges among the supervisors of banks, securities firms, and insurance companies.

---

[113]See Chapter VIII.

Location of the Banking Supervision Function

Different traditions and systems exist for locating the banking supervisory function inside or outside the central bank.[116] Whichever institutional arrangement is chosen, it is of key importance for the effectiveness of banking supervision that the position of the supervisory authority be especially circumscribed in law and that a minimum set of institutional conditions be met, as described above (such as independence from political pressure, adequate coordination of banking supervision and monetary policy, and adequate staffing and resources). If these conditions are met, the location of the supervisory function becomes less relevant for practical purposes, although the autonomy and independence of the supervisory authority may be easier to maintain in countries with relatively weak institutional structures when the supervisory function is located in the central bank than when it is a separate agency. This is particularly true when the central bank itself has a high degree of autonomy and independence.[117]

Off-Site Analysis and On-Site Inspections

Banking supervision requires off-site monitoring and analysis as well as on-site inspections of banks' records, operations, and management. While the balance between on-site inspection and off-site supervision can vary considerably between countries, the supervisory authority needs to have both the right to require production of whatever information it needs and the right to conduct on-site inspections. The verification of the reliability of the reported information, its accurate reflection of the risks, the quality of assets, and the effectiveness of management and internal controls can only be effectively tested by intensive and well-targeted on-site inspections.[118] This can also provide indications on the effectiveness of external audits. The supervisors' inspections should encourage management to take appropriate precautions against imprudent transactions, and should support internal systems that prevent excessively risky transactions.

Periodic prudential reports are the basis for the off-site analysis of the condition of the bank. Off-site reports can also be used as input for an early warning system.[119] Noncompliance and submission of false or incomplete data are a punishable offence. Effective supervisors are also authorized to obtain from the bank any additional information they consider necessary for effective supervision. In addition to reports, off-site information could consist of a permanent file on the management and organization of the bank, as well as a collection of the bank's financial statements and articles of association, and an operational file on the contacts between the bank and the supervisory authorities, including records of any remedial measures that have been prescribed and taken and any permissions that have been granted or refused pursuant to prudential requirements.

On-site inspections are typically based on the following operational principles:

- A comprehensive on-site inspection program is prepared for each bank, setting out the coverage, time frame, and periodicity of the inspections. On-site inspections are announced in advance, unless there is a suspicion of fraud or bad faith.
- Inspections focus on asset quality, management, and risk-management systems, as well as on formal compliance with regulations.
- Inspectors use off-site data, results of previous inspections, market information, and other sources as the input for inspections. Inspectors should also have access to any information and staff, specifically including the internal and external auditors and their reports.
- The supervisory authority should know the institution well, including its business and its key staff, and build a relationship of trust and professional respect with the individual banks. The bank must feel free to discuss problems openly and in full confidence, without fear of provoking measures by other public agencies.
- Prudential on-site inspections are carried out solely by supervisory staff or by other qualified persons designated by the supervisory authority.
- An inspection is followed up within a specified time by a report to the management and the board of the bank to ensure that any problems are addressed. Conferences between the bank and the supervisory authorities to discuss the results of the inspection are a useful supervisory tool.
- The report contains proposals for prompt remedial measures and proactive recommendations, as appropriate. Follow-up inspections may be needed to monitor implementation.
- When dealing with branches or subsidiaries of foreign banks, the supervisory authorities must have as much access as possible to establishments of its banks abroad, allow access to foreign supervisors, and establish general good working contacts with the foreign supervisory authority (see Chapter VIII).

---

[116]For a discussion of the question whether the supervisory function should be located inside or outside the central bank, see Tuya and Zamalloa (1994).

[117]Similarly, if the supervisory authority were to be based in a different institution, the autonomy and independence of that institution should be assured.

[118]In some countries, on-site inspection is carried out by auditors acting under the specific instructions of the supervisory authority.

[119]The content of such reports is described in detail in Chapter IV.

Remedial and Punitive Measures

Supervisory authorities need a flexible range of remedial and punitive measures to correct unsafe or unsound banking practices and to punish transgressions.[120] Remedial actions are intended to improve the bank's operations before the problem becomes insurmountable, while punitive actions are designed to deter management from breaches of the regulations and from unsafe and unsound banking practices. These measures represent a backstop when market discipline cannot, perhaps due to insufficient information, or does not operate effectively.

The supervisory authorities need to be able to tailor their response to the seriousness of the problem. Whenever possible, the initial actions would be remedial. The supervisor would start by drawing attention to shortcomings and requesting management's written commitment to take corrective action. In more severe cases, when a more formal arrangement is appropriate, an exchange of letters between the bank and the supervisory authorities could be used. When compliance is inadequate, a next step could be a written warning by the supervisory authorities stating that they will take formal action if the bank does not take corrective action against specified breaches or unsafe and unsound banking practices.

Supervisory actions need to be carefully prepared and implemented, especially when they are not legally enforceable, to establish a track record against a bank, in order to defend such actions in a court of law or, possibly, before the political authorities. A track record of action should also lay the groundwork for possible further supervisory action, such as conservatorship or license withdrawal. The bank must never be in a position to claim that it had not been informed of the seriousness of the supervisors' view of the situation, except, of course, in rapidly developing cases or in cases of fraud.

The supervisory authorities also need to be able to take legally binding action to enforce compliance with specific remedial measures. Such actions could consist of a "cease and desist" order, ordering a bank to improve operations or close or limit deposit-taking or certain types of credit business, or other actions to correct specific breaches or unsafe and unsound practices. A next step could be a dismissal order against a director or manager who can no longer be considered fit and proper, as a result of major management failings or refusal to comply with corrective orders. In some cases, punitive measures such as fines levied against the manager or director personally can be effective. The most effective measures are those tailored toward remedying the deficiency. For instance, when capital is below the required level, a first step could be to prohibit dividend payments. The banking law normally specifies that noncompliance with a corrective order or dismissal order is a punishable offense, potentially subject to action by the prosecuting authorities, and leading to substantial fines or prison sentences.

As measures of last resort, but in urgent cases also as a first measure, when the financial condition of the bank has deteriorated to a potentially terminal level or there is evidence of serious criminal activity sanctioned by management, the supervisory authorities would have the authority to impose conservatorship or withdraw the license, to rehabilitate the bank or force its closure and liquidation.

---

[120]See Supervision Guideline No. 13, "Enforcement" in World Bank (1992).

VIII

Cross-Border Supervision of Banks

This chapter discusses international aspects of maintaining banking soundness. It identifies some of the key problem issues in supervising banks and banking groups with cross-border operations, that is, the location of the home supervisor, licensing of internationally active banks and their establishments and affiliates abroad, cross-border compliance with prudential standards, information flows, inspections, cross-border remedial action, shell banks and parallel-owned banks, international financial conglomerates, and international bank liquidation.

Evolution of Best Practices

The key challenge for supervisory authorities of internationally active banks has been to ensure that no activity of these banks escapes effective supervision and that coordinated remedial action can be undertaken when necessary. These challenges have become more salient over the past few years. Banks in industrialized countries have expanded their business into emerging and transitional economies, using their comparative advantages in producing and distributing financial services. Banks in emerging and transitional economies have, but to a much lesser extent, expanded their activities in the industrialized countries, other emerging-market countries, and offshore banking centers as they attempt to meet the competition from the major banks and take advantage of increased opportunities made possible by the relaxation of domestic regulation.

The cross-border expansion of banks can be expected in general to increase the efficiency of global capital markets, as the entrance of highly rated foreign banks frequently spurs competition among the domestic banks. However, cross-border expansion can create a variety of difficulties for supervision. This is particularly true for emerging market countries that are still developing their accounting or legal systems, and where supervisory resources are limited. First, as evidenced by the well-known case of BCCI and the lesser-known case of the Meridien International Bank, the creation of various types of corporate structures across international borders can be used to escape regulation and effective supervision. Second, the growing ability of and propensity for banks to shift their activities to offshore tax havens present a channel whereby domestic prudential regulations can be easily circumvented. Third, when accounting practices are relatively unsophisticated and disclosure laws are limited, cross-border transactions can be used to conceal problems at domestic financial institutions by booking problem assets with subsidiaries or other offshore entities. Finally, offshore transactions can be used to facilitate or commit outright fraud. Incentives for prudent behavior are varied across different jurisdictions, leading some institutions to seek out countries in which high-risk activities go unnoticed.

The circumvention of domestic prudential regulations, in particular underreporting of nonperforming assets through offshore entities, increases the risks taken by the bank or banking group as a whole and implies that bank capital may be insufficient. Fraudulent activities that are hidden by relocation to underregulated cross-border establishments create losses that will ultimately have to be borne domestically. While supervising banking establishments across borders can be difficult and strain meager resources, the cost of not adequately doing so could, in the end, be greater.

Basic principles and standards on a number of aspects of supervision and regulation of cross-border banking have been developed by the Basle Committee on Banking Supervision, starting with the so-called Basle Concordat in 1975 (see Basle Committee, 1975 and 1983). Implementation of the principles in the Concordat was for many years on a best endeavors basis. Following the BCCI failure, the Basle Committee issued its "Minimum Standards" in 1992 (see Box 7), underlining and further developing some of the main concepts of the Concordat with regard to cross-border supervision (see Basle Committee, 1992). To implement the standards, a number of countries have concluded bilateral exchanges of letters or signed Memoranda of Understanding.[121] Subsequently, a working group of the Basle Committee and the Offshore Group of Banking Supervisors is seeking to resolve a number of issues relating to the implementation of the minimum standards, and has recently

---

[121]See the Office of the Comptroller of the Currency (1996), for example, describing supervisory agreements between the United States and Germany.

issued a set of recommendations to supplement the minimum standards.[122]

Current Status of Best Practices

This section discusses contacts and cooperation between a home and a single host supervisor based on the principles mentioned above.

Location of the Licensing and Lead Supervisory Authority

A home-country supervisory authority is responsible for supervising the global operations of a bank or banking group, on the basis of consolidated and verifiable financial and prudential information. This approach encompasses not only a bank holding company's or parent bank's direct branches and subsidiaries, but also includes any significant nonbank companies and financial affiliates.

The home country should also be the location of the senior management and the bulk (the majority of the consolidated balance sheet total) of a bank's business. If the majority of the activities appear to be conducted

elsewhere, it would become difficult for the home supervisor to fulfill its obligations, and arrangements should be made with another country involved to take on the role of home supervisor. The case of BCCI, where the licensing authorities for the two parent banks could only supervise a very minor part of the group's activities, as the bulk was conducted in other jurisdictions, has illustrated the necessity of this approach.

Licensing of Internationally Active Banks

Home and host authorities should both give their explicit permission for the setting up of an establishment abroad (see Basle Committee, 1992). The home authority should be able to refuse the establishment of a branch or subsidiary of a bank jurisdiction, suspected to be inadequately regulated. In addition to applying normal licensing procedure to a foreign bank, home- and host-country authorities should also consider the bank's and banking group's organization and operating procedures for the management of risks, internal controls, and audits, on both a domestic and cross-border basis. In judging these criteria, a host-country authority should be particularly concerned with the level of support that the head office or parent is capable of providing to the proposed establishment.

Before granting consent to the establishment of a cross-border establishment, the home and host authorities should each review their supervisory responsibilities with respect to the establishment. If either of the authorities has any concerns about the division of responsibilities, then that authority has the responsibility to initiate consultations with the other authority so that they reach an explicit understanding on which one of them is in the best position to take primary responsibility either generally or in respect of specific activities. A similar review should be undertaken by both authorities if there is a significant change in the bank's or banking group's activities or structure.

International Implementation of Prudential Standards

The home-country supervisory authority has responsibility for supervising the bank or banking group on a consolidated basis, domestically as well as internationally. The home supervisor will also need to take account of the fact that capital cannot always easily be moved from one part of a banking group to another across international borders. Host countries are primarily responsible for the liquidity of a foreign establishment, since they will be better equipped to assess liquidity as a function of local market conditions and practices and the establishment's position in the market.[123] But they will also be responsible for the sol-

---

[122]See Basle Committee (1996c). Also included in the Basle Committee's *Compendium of Documents* (1997b).

[123]See Basle Committee (1983).

vency and supervision of subsidiaries. The Basle Concordat and its subsequent amendments and additions set out the respective responsibilities of host and home authorities. Host authorities are responsible for the foreign bank establishments in their territory, and home-country authorities are responsible for these establishments as parts of larger-scale activities of banks under their supervision. Notwithstanding a certain division of labor, home and host authorities need to be in close contact and cooperate effectively.

Cross-Border Supervisory Information

Home country supervisors have the right to gather information from their cross-border banking establishments. Host authorities should be able to obtain any necessary information from the home authority. This ability to gather information should be a condition for giving consent for the cross-border establishment of a bank, although appropriate safeguards for confidentiality are necessary. Any undue impediments in the home and the host country in the area of bank secrecy and confidentiality to the exchange of supervisory information between banking supervisory authorities should be removed (see Basle Committee, 1983). At the same time, legal arrangements need to be in place to safeguard the information that has been exchanged, especially relating to depositors', creditors', or investors' names, against disclosure to third parties. Local supervisory authorities should provide access to the local establishment of a bank to auditors of the head office or parent corporation and be willing to discuss the affairs of the local establishment with the auditor.

The information to be shared should include both quantitative and qualitative aspects, including balance sheets, income or profit and loss accounts, information on shareholders and management, internal control systems, internal audit, external auditors' reports, prudential reports, and any other information that can be considered necessary for the proper exercise of supervision.[124] The information should permit the supervisors to calculate the bank's (or banking group's) capital adequacy ratios, large exposures or legal lending limits, and funding and deposit concentrations on a consolidated basis. Even if from an accounting point of view full consolidation is technically not possible, the home and host supervisors should be able to verify the network of the bank's other affiliations or branches, financial or nonfinancial, as well as the transactions between these entities. Home and host authorities will need to be aware that prudential standards and supervisory practices may differ between countries.

Information on individual clients of a bank will typically have the highest degree of confidentiality protection. Such information will be required when assessing asset quality and credit files may need to be examined. However, when a supervisor detects a serious crime during an inspection or analysis of off-site data, law enforcement agencies and the supervisors in other countries involved should be informed as quickly as possible. Information on substantial changes in strategy, ownership, financial situation, or any problems in establishments abroad, head offices, or parent banks should be communicated immediately to the other supervisory authorities involved.

Cross-Border Inspections

Authorities of the host state should permit on-site inspections by the home supervisor of a prudential nature[125] of establishments of internationally active banks within its jurisdiction. Together with the free flow of data, such inspections are a necessary corollary of effective consolidated supervision.

The conduct of on-site inspections on the territory of another state requires the consent of the country receiving the inspection team. Any legal barriers against such on-site inspections would need to be removed, for instance by concluding agreements between countries on the conduct of such inspections. Such agreements should preferably be multilateral in the case of banks active in several jurisdictions. If legal impediments exist in the interim, host supervisors should be willing to cooperate to the fullest extent possible, within the limits of their laws, with any home supervisor that wishes to make an inspection. This can be facilitated by allowing the host supervisor the option to accompany the home supervisor throughout the inspection.

Operational aspects of cross-border inspections would typically need to be agreed upon in advance by both authorities. For this, standardized arrangements could be made between the supervisory authorities.[126] The findings of inspections should be shared between the supervisory authorities of both countries, as well as with the institution involved.

Supervisory Action Against Establishments Abroad

When inspections or other information would indicate the need for remedial or punitive action, this may be complicated by differences in the legal arrange-

---

[124]See Chapter IV for a complete discussion of the information requirements for supervisors.

[125]In some countries, on-site inspections are used to verify compliance with nonprudential rules and regulations, such as taxation laws; inspections teams often include, for example, investigative staff of taxation authorities and law enforcement agencies.

[126]See, for instance, the supervisory arrangements between the United States and Germany described in Office of the Comptroller of the Currency (1996).

ments. Supervisory authorities in different countries should therefore conclude arrangements to make supervisory action in the foreign state possible, should the need arise. These arrangements could also include providing assistance in accessing local nonsupervisory information, for example, on the legal system, on shareholders' activities, and in obtaining good legal counsel.

Branches abroad are the responsibility of the head office. Therefore, the home country supervisor can require the management at the head office to remedy deficiencies in the branches, and apply the full range of legal instruments against the head office to achieve this result. Subsidiaries should also be subject to consolidated supervision, but are subject to the jurisdiction of the host state. The parent bank is likely to have considerable influence and its home supervisor may use this influence to induce improvements.

Information on Supervisory Systems and Structures

A host state should be able to ascertain whether the home state can "capably perform home country consolidated supervision" (see Basle Committee, 1992) as a condition for permitting an establishment of a foreign bank entry to its territory. If the host supervisory authority is in any doubt in this respect, it should either refuse entry, or stipulate that the establishment shall be supervised on a strict "stand-alone" basis. The host and home authorities should in any case be well aware of each other's supervisory systems and practices. The supervisory authorities of both states should exchange complete information on each other's banking laws, the scope of their respective authorities, and prudential regulations applicable to the establishment on their territory. The supervisory authority should have adequate powers to obtain the necessary information, including regular financial reports and prudential reports. The quantity and quality of available resources to supervise the foreign operation should be assessed, as well as supervisory techniques, frequency of inspections, et cetera. These items should provide the basis for a judgment as to whether the supervisory authority is capable of performing consolidated supervision. It is also important to establish the track record of the other supervisory authority in taking effective supervisory action against banks, especially those with establishments abroad.

To facilitate the process, a system of routine personal contacts should be set up between supervisors of the host and home countries, including the exchange of names, addresses, and information on language and other skills. Such information is crucial for building a good and effective working relationship between both authorities and for taking action when necessary. It will greatly facilitate many of the aspects of cross-border supervision as described above.

"Shell Banks" and Parallel-Owned Banks[127]

The authority that licenses a so-called shell bank, defined here as a loan generation or booking office, licensed or registered in one center but effectively controlled or managed from another jurisdiction, has responsibility for supervising the shell bank. To be effective, no shell bank should be licensed if the head office in another jurisdiction is not subject to adequate banking supervision on a consolidated basis. When a license is requested for a shell bank, the supervisory authority needs to establish contact with the home supervisor of the bank or its parent bank and ascertain whether permission has been granted to open the office abroad. Only when all necessary information on the bank and on the quality of home-country supervision is obtained and found satisfactory can the application be approved.

The home supervisor needs to be allowed to inspect the books of the shell bank wherever they are kept, and in whatever form, in order to establish whether banking activities are undertaken and whether the risks are adequately controlled by the head office. If the home supervisor is not allowed to conduct an inspection, it cannot authorize the shell bank to be established. If, subsequent to its opening, the home supervisor is unable to satisfactorily inspect the books, the shell bank must be closed.

Parallel-owned banks, where a bank in one jurisdiction is under the same nonbank ownership as a bank in another jurisdiction, are more problematic and need to be kept under close scrutiny. If the nonbank owner has as its sole activity the ownership of one or more banks, the owner ought to also be subject to the consolidated banking supervision of a single banking supervisory authority, notwithstanding the separate responsibility of the supervisory authorities in the respective individual countries. In the absence of such an arrangement, it will be necessary for the respective supervisors to prevent sources of contagion, for example by particularly rigorous connected lending rules.

International Financial Conglomerates

The problems illustrated above become even more salient in the case of an internationally active financial conglomerate. Supervisors over conglomerates active in several financial sectors need to establish close contacts and make practical arrangements for the exercise of supervision. A financial group, incorporating banking, securities, and insurance subsidiaries and other financial intermediaries, can be subject to three or more different regulators and regulatory regimes. At the domestic level, this already poses significant problems of coordination, information, and compliance with

---

[127]See Basle Committee (1996c).

prudential regulations. These problems are compounded at the international level, where the problem of coordination, information, and compliance potentially involves several regulators for each country in which the conglomerate is active. In such cases, some countries have found it useful to designate lead regulators to carry out a coordinating role.

The technical issues that need to be addressed in the context of international financial conglomerates have been enumerated in the Joint Forum's mandate, and consist of (1) the supervision of financial conglomerates on a groupwide perspective; (2) techniques for assessing the adequacy of capital of financial conglomerates; (3) supervisors' ability to check on fit and proper standards of managers and their ability to ensure that shareholders meet adequate standards; (4) the supervisory approach to participation of less than 100 percent in entities within financial conglomerates; (5) the supervisory approach to large exposures and to intragroup exposures within financial conglomerates; and (6) the supervisors' ability to intervene in structures that impair effective supervision.

International Bank Liquidation[128]

When a bank that has a branch in another country is closed, liquidated, or declared insolvent, the supervisory authority in the country where the branch is established must immediately be informed by the home supervisory authority. The host authority would then promptly close the branch. Any additional liabilities incurred by the branch, for instance, would fall within the estate of the closed bank. Subsidiaries are legally separate from the parent bank. Their assets and liabil-

ities in theory remain unchanged when the parent bank closes. However, there is an increased risk of uploading or downloading assets and liabilities between the closed parent and the subsidiary, which could damage the subsidiary's depositors and other creditors.

Ideally, bank liquidation takes place on the basis of a single set of rules. In practice, international bank insolvencies are extremely complicated, as some countries follow the separate-entity approach and are able to place their depositors and creditors before those of other countries, irrespective of liquidation law in the other country, whereas other countries follow the single-entity approach, which considers the bank as a whole and gives equal treatment to all creditors wherever their domicile and whether their claim is on a domestic or foreign branch. These are issues that cannot be solved by supervisors, even when the outcome is relevant to the proper execution of their task. In the light of the greater internationalization of banking activities and the potential international impact of such liquidations, further international harmonization of insolvency rules for financial institutions is desirable.[129] Work on international insolvency law is being undertaken by the United Nations Commission on International Trade Law (UNCITRAL), and recently a draft document of the Group of Thirty was issued on international insolvencies of financial institutions.[130] It is essential that supervisory authorities keep each other closely informed on bank insolvencies and liquidations, and provide all possible assistance in giving foreign supervisors access to the proceedings in their countries.

---

[128]The Core Principles for Effective Banking Supervision do not address international bank liquidation.

[129]See Basle Committee (1993), which discusses problems associated with the liquidation of BCCI.

[130]Group of Thirty (1996). The European Union has for many years attempted to reach agreement on rules for the intervention in and liquidation of banks.

Annex I

Core Principles for Effective Banking Supervision[1] (Basle Core Principles)

1. Weaknesses in the banking system of a country, whether developing or developed, can threaten financial stability both within that country and internationally. The need to **improve the strength of financial systems** has attracted growing international concern. The Communiqué issued at the close of the Lyon G-7 Summit in June 1996 called for action in this domain. Several official bodies, including the Basle Committee on Banking Supervision, the Bank for International Settlements, the International Monetary Fund and the World Bank, have recently been examining ways to strengthen financial stability throughout the world.

2. The Basle Committee on Banking Supervision[2] has been working in this field for many years, both directly and through its many contacts with banking supervisors in every part of the world. In the last year and a half, it has been examining how best to expand its efforts aimed at strengthening prudential supervision in all countries by building on its relationships with countries outside the G-10 as well as on its earlier work to enhance prudential supervision in its member countries. In particular, the Committee has prepared two documents for release:

- a comprehensive set of **Core Principles** for effective banking supervision (The Basle Core Principles) (attached); and
- a **Compendium** (to be updated periodically) of the existing Basle Committee recommendations, guidelines and standards most of which are cross-referenced in the Core Principles document.

Both documents have been endorsed by the G-10 central bank Governors. They were submitted to the G-7 and G-10 Finance Ministers in preparation for the June 1997 Denver Summit in the hope that they would provide a useful mechanism for strengthening financial stability in all countries.

3. In developing the Principles, the Basle Committee has worked closely with **non-G-10 supervisory authorities**. The document has been prepared in a group containing representatives from the Basle Committee and from Chile, China, the Czech Republic, Hong Kong, Mexico, Russia and Thailand. Nine other countries (Argentina, Brazil, Hungary, India, Indonesia, Korea, Malaysia, Poland and Singapore) were also closely associated with the work. The drafting of the Principles benefited moreover from broad consultation with a larger group of individual supervisors, both directly and through the regional supervisory groups.

4. The Basle Core Principles comprise **twenty-five basic Principles** that need to be in place for a supervisory system to be effective. The Principles relate to:

Preconditions for effective banking supervision—Principle 1
Licensing and structure—Principles 2 to 5
Prudential regulations and requirements—Principles 6 to 15
Methods of ongoing banking supervision—Principles 16 to 20
Information requirements—Principle 21
Formal powers of supervisors—Principle 22, and
Cross-border banking—Principles 23 to 25.

In addition to the Principles themselves, the document contains explanations of the various methods supervisors can use to implement them.

5. National agencies should apply the Principles in the supervision of all banking organisations within their jurisdictions.[3] The Principles are **minimum requirements** and in many cases may need to be supplemented by other measures designed to address particular conditions and risks in the financial systems of individual countries.

6. The Basle Core Principles are intended to serve as a basic reference for **supervisory and other public**

---

[1]Basle Committee on Banking Supervision, Basle, September 1997.

[2]The Basle Committee on Banking Supervision is a Committee of banking supervisory authorities which was established by the central bank Governors of the Group of Ten countries in 1975. It consists of senior representatives of banking supervisory authorities and central banks from Belgium, Canada, France, Germany, Italy, Japan, Luxembourg, Netherlands, Sweden, Switzerland, United Kingdom and the United States. It usually meets at the Bank for International Settlements in Basle, where its permanent Secretariat is located.

---

[3]In countries where non-bank financial institutions provide financial services similar to those of banks, many of the Principles set out in this document are also capable of application to such non-bank financial institutions.

authorities in all countries and internationally. It will be for national supervisory authorities, many of which are actively seeking to strengthen their current supervisory regime, to use the attached document to review their existing supervisory arrangements and to initiate a programme designed to address any deficiencies as quickly as is practical within their legal authority. The Principles have been designed to be verifiable by supervisors, regional supervisory groups, and the market at large. The Basle Committee will play a role, together with other interested organisations, in monitoring the progress made by individual countries in implementing the Principles. It is suggested that the IMF, the World Bank and other interested organisations use the Principles in assisting individual countries to strengthen their supervisory arrangements in connection with work aimed at promoting overall macroeconomic and financial stability. Implementation of the Principles will be reviewed at the International Conference of Banking Supervisors in October 1998 and biennially thereafter.

7. Supervisory authorities throughout the world are encouraged to **endorse** the Basle Core Principles. The members of the Basle Committee and the sixteen other supervisory agencies that have participated in their drafting all agree with the content of the document.

8. The chairpersons of the **regional supervisory groups**[4] are supportive of the Basle Committee's efforts and are ready to promote the endorsement of the Core Principles among their membership. Discussions are in progress to define the role the regional groups can play in securing the endorsement of the Principles and in monitoring implementation by their members.

9. The Basle Committee believes that achieving consistency with the Core Principles by every country will be a significant step in the process of improving financial stability domestically and internationally. The speed with which this objective will be achieved will vary. In many countries, substantive **changes in the legislative framework** and in the powers of supervisors will be necessary because many supervisory authorities do not at present have the statutory authority to implement all of the Principles. In such cases, the Basle Committee believes it is essential that national legislators give urgent consideration to the changes necessary to ensure that the Principles can be applied in all material respects.

---

[4]Arab Committee on Banking Supervision, Caribbean Banking Supervisors Group, Association of Banking Supervisory Authorities of Latin America and the Caribbean, Eastern and Southern Africa Banking Supervisors Group, EMEAP Study Group on Banking Supervision, Group of Banking Supervisors from Central and Eastern European Countries, Gulf Cooperation Council Banking Supervisors' Committee, Offshore Group of Banking Supervisors, Regional Supervisory Group of Central Asia and Transcaucasia, SEANZA Forum of Banking Supervisors, Committee of Banking Supervisors in West and Central Africa.

10. **The Basle Committee** will continue to pursue its standard-setting activities in key risk areas and in key elements of banking supervision as it has done in documents such as those reproduced in the Compendium. The Basle Core Principles will serve as a reference point for future work to be done by the Committee and, where appropriate, in cooperation with non-G-10 supervisors and their regional groups. The Committee stands ready to encourage work at the national level to implement the Principles in conjunction with other supervisory bodies and interested parties. Finally, the Committee is committed to strengthening its interaction with supervisors from non-G-10 countries and intensifying its considerable investment in technical assistance and training.

List of Core Principles for Effective Banking Supervision

Preconditions for Effective Banking Supervision

1. An effective system of banking supervision will have clear responsibilities and objectives for each agency involved in the supervision of banking organisations. Each such agency should possess operational independence and adequate resources. A suitable legal framework for banking supervision is also necessary, including provisions relating to authorisation of banking organisations and their ongoing supervision; powers to address compliance with laws as well as safety and soundness concerns; and legal protection for supervisors. Arrangements for sharing information between supervisors and protecting the confidentiality of such information should be in place.

Licensing and Structure

2. The permissible activities of institutions that are licensed and subject to supervision as banks must be clearly defined, and the use of the word "bank" in names should be controlled as far as possible.

3. The licensing authority must have the right to set criteria and reject applications for establishments that do not meet the standards set. The licensing process, at a minimum, should consist of an assessment of the banking organisation's ownership structure, directors and senior management, its operating plan and internal controls, and its projected financial condition, including its capital base; where the proposed owner or parent organisation is a foreign bank, the prior consent of its home country supervisor should be obtained.

4. Banking supervisors must have the authority to review and reject any proposals to transfer significant ownership or controlling interests in existing banks to other parties.

5. Banking supervisors must have the authority to establish criteria for reviewing major acquisitions or

investments by a bank and ensuring that corporate affiliations or structures do not expose the bank to undue risks or hinder effective supervision.

Prudential Regulations and Requirements

6. Banking supervisors must set prudent and appropriate minimum capital adequacy requirements for all banks. Such requirements should reflect the risks that the banks undertake, and must define the components of capital, bearing in mind their ability to absorb losses. At least for internationally active banks, these requirements must not be less than those established in the Basle Capital Accord and its amendments.

7. An essential part of any supervisory system is the evaluation of a bank's policies, practices and procedures related to the granting of loans and making of investments and the ongoing management of the loan and investment portfolios.

8. Banking supervisors must be satisfied that banks establish and adhere to adequate policies, practices and procedures for evaluating the quality of assets and the adequacy of loan loss provisions and loan loss reserves.

9. Banking supervisors must be satisfied that banks have management information systems that enable management to identify concentrations within the portfolio and supervisors must set prudential limits to restrict bank exposures to single borrowers or groups of related borrowers.

10. In order to prevent abuses arising from connected lending, banking supervisors must have in place requirements that banks lend to related companies and individuals on an arm's-length basis, that such extensions of credit are effectively monitored, and that other appropriate steps are taken to control or mitigate the risks.

11. Banking supervisors must be satisfied that banks have adequate policies and procedures for identifying, monitoring and controlling country risk and transfer risk in their international lending and investment activities, and for maintaining appropriate reserves against such risks.

12. Banking supervisors must be satisfied that banks have in place systems that accurately measure, monitor and adequately control market risks; supervisors should have powers to impose specific limits and/or a specific capital charge on market risk exposures, if warranted.

13. Banking supervisors must be satisfied that banks have in place a comprehensive risk management process (including appropriate board and senior management oversight) to identify, measure, monitor and control all other material risks and, where appropriate, to hold capital against these risks.

14. Banking supervisors must determine that banks have in place internal controls that are adequate for the nature and scale of their business. These should include clear arrangements for delegating authority and responsibility; separation of the functions that involve committing the bank, paying away its funds, and accounting for its assets and liabilities; reconciliation of these processes; safeguarding its assets; and appropriate independent internal or external audit and compliance functions to test adherence to these controls as well as applicable laws and regulations.

15. Banking supervisors must determine that banks have adequate policies, practices and procedures in place, including strict "know-your-customer" rules, that promote high ethical and professional standards in the financial sector and prevent the bank being used, intentionally or unintentionally, by criminal elements.

Methods of Ongoing Banking Supervision

16. An effective banking supervisory system should consist of some form of both on-site and off-site supervision.

17. Banking supervisors must have regular contact with bank management and thorough understanding of the institution's operations.

18. Banking supervisors must have a means of collecting, reviewing and analysing prudential reports and statistical returns from banks on a solo and consolidated basis.

19. Banking supervisors must have a means of independent validation of supervisory information either through on-site examinations or use of external auditors.

20. An essential element of banking supervision is the ability of the supervisors to supervise the banking group on a consolidated basis.

Information Requirements

21. Banking supervisors must be satisfied that each bank maintains adequate records drawn up in accordance with consistent accounting policies and practices that enable the supervisor to obtain a true and fair view of the financial condition of the bank and the profitability of its business, and that the bank publishes on a regular basis financial statements that fairly reflect its condition.

Formal Powers of Supervisors

22. Banking supervisors must have at their disposal adequate supervisory measures to bring about timely corrective action when banks fail to meet prudential requirements (such as minimum capital adequacy ratios), when there are regulatory violations, or where depositors are threatened in any other way. In extreme circumstances, this should include the ability to revoke the banking licence or recommend its revocation.

Cross-Border Banking

23. Banking supervisors must practise global consolidated supervision over their internationally-active banking organisations, adequately monitoring and applying appropriate prudential norms to all aspects of the business conducted by these banking organisations worldwide, primarily at their foreign branches, joint ventures and subsidiaries.

24. A key component of consolidated supervision is establishing contact and information exchange with the various other supervisors involved, primarily host country supervisory authorities.

25. Banking supervisors must require the local operations of foreign banks to be conducted to the same high standards as are required of domestic institutions and must have powers to share information needed by the home country supervisors of those banks for the purpose of carrying out consolidated supervision.

Section I: Introduction

Effective supervision of banking organisations is an essential component of a strong economic environment in that the banking system plays a central role in making payments and mobilising and distributing savings. The task of supervision is to ensure that banks operate in a safe and sound manner and that they hold capital and reserves sufficient to support the risks that arise in their business. Strong and effective banking supervision provides a public good that may not be fully provided in the marketplace and, along with effective macroeconomic policy, is critical to financial stability in any country. While the cost of banking supervision is indeed high, the cost of poor supervision has proved to be even higher.

In drawing up these core principles for effective banking supervision the following precepts are fundamental:

- the key objective of supervision is to maintain stability and confidence in the financial system, thereby reducing the risk of loss to depositors and other creditors;
- supervisors should encourage and pursue market discipline by encouraging good corporate governance (through an appropriate structure and set of responsibilities for a bank's board of directors and senior management)[5] and enhancing market transparency and surveillance;

- in order to carry out its tasks effectively, a supervisor must have operational independence, the means and powers to gather information both on and off site, and the authority to enforce its decisions;
- supervisors must understand the nature of the business undertaken by banks and ensure to the extent possible that the risks incurred by banks are being adequately managed;
- effective banking supervision requires that the risk profile of individual banks be assessed and supervisory resources allocated accordingly;
- supervisors must ensure that banks have resources appropriate to undertake risks, including adequate capital, sound management, and effective control systems and accounting records; and
- close cooperation with other supervisors is essential, particularly where the operations of banking organisations cross national boundaries.

Banking supervision should foster an efficient and competitive banking system that is responsive to the public's need for good quality financial services at a reasonable cost. Generally, it should be recognised that there is a trade-off between the level of protection that supervision provides and the cost of financial intermediation. The lower the tolerance of risk to banks and the financial system, the more intrusive and costly supervision is likely to be, eventually having an adverse effect on innovation and resource allocation.

Supervision cannot, and should not, provide an assurance that banks will not fail. In a market economy, failures are a part of risk-taking. The way in which failures are handled, and their costs borne, is in large part a political matter involving decisions on whether, and the extent to which, public funds should be committed to supporting the banking system. Such matters cannot therefore always be entirely the responsibility of banking supervisors; however, supervisors should have in place adequate arrangements for resolving problem bank situations.

There are certain infrastructure elements that are required to support effective supervision. Where such elements do not exist, supervisors should seek to persuade government to put them in place (and may have a role in designing and developing them). These elements are discussed in Section II.

In some countries responsibility for licensing banks is separate from the process of ongoing supervision. It is clearly essential that, wherever the responsibility

---

[5]This document refers to a management structure composed of a board of directors and senior management. The Committee is aware that there are significant differences in legislative and regulatory frameworks across countries as regards the functions of the board of directors and senior management. In some countries, the board has the main, if not exclusive, function of supervising the executive body (senior management, general management) so as to ensure that the latter fulfils its tasks. For this reason, in some

cases, it is known as a supervisory board. This means that the board has no executive functions. In other countries, by contrast, the board has a broader competence in that it lays down the general framework for the management of the bank. Owing to these differences, the notions of the board of directors and the senior management are used in this document not to identify legal constructs but rather to label two decision-making functions within a bank.

lies, the licensing process establishes the same high standards as the process of ongoing supervision which is the main focus of this paper. Section III therefore discusses some principles and issues that should be addressed in the licensing process.

The core principles of banking supervision set out above and expanded in Sections III–VI of this document will provide the foundation necessary to achieve a sound supervisory system. Local characteristics will need to be taken into account in the specific way in which these standards are implemented. These standards are necessary but may not be sufficient, on their own, in all situations. Supervisory systems should take into account the nature of and risks involved in the local banking market as well as more generally the local infrastructure. Each country should therefore consider to what extent it needs to supplement these standards with additional requirements to address particular risks and general conditions prevailing in its own market. Furthermore, banking supervision is a dynamic function that needs to respond to changes in the marketplace. Consequently supervisors must be prepared to reassess periodically their supervisory policies and practices in the light of new trends or developments. A sufficiently flexible legislative framework is necessary to enable them to do this.

Section II: Preconditions for Effective Banking Supervision

Banking supervision is only part of wider arrangements that are needed to promote stability in financial markets. These arrangements include:

1. sound and sustainable macro-economic policies;
2. a well developed public infrastructure;
3. effective market discipline;
4. procedures for efficient resolution of problems in banks; and
5. mechanisms for providing an appropriate level of systemic protection (or public safety net).

1. *Providing sound and sustainable macro-economic policies* is not within the competence of banking supervisors. Supervisors, however, will need to react if they perceive that existing policies are undermining the safety and soundness of the banking system. In the absence of sound macro-economic policies, banking supervisors will be faced with a virtually impossible task. Therefore, sound macro-economic policies must be the foundation of a stable financial system.

2. *A well developed public infrastructure* needs to cover the following facilities, which, if not adequately provided, can significantly contribute to the destabilisation of financial systems:

- a system of business laws including corporate, bankruptcy, contract, consumer protection and private property laws that is consistently enforced and provides a mechanism for fair resolution of disputes;
- comprehensive and well-defined accounting principles and rules that command wide international acceptance;
- a system of independent audits for companies of significant size so that users of financial statements, including banks, have independent assurance that the accounts provide a true and fair view of the financial position of the company and are prepared according to established accounting principles, with auditors held accountable for their work;
- effective banking supervision (as outlined in this document);
- well-defined rules governing, and adequate supervision of, other financial markets and, where appropriate, their participants; and
- a secure and efficient payment and clearing system for the settlement of financial transactions where counterparty risks are controlled.

3. *Effective market discipline* depends on an adequate flow of information to market participants, appropriate financial incentives to reward well managed institutions and arrangements that ensure that investors are not insulated from the consequences of their decisions. Among the issues to be addressed are corporate governance and ensuring that accurate, meaningful, transparent and timely information is provided by borrowers to investors and creditors.

Market signals can be distorted and discipline undermined if governments seek to influence or override commercial decisions, particularly lending decisions, to achieve public policy objectives. In these circumstances, it is important that if guarantees are provided for such lending, they are disclosed and arrangements are made to compensate financial institutions when policy loans cease to perform.

4. Sufficiently flexible powers are necessary in order to effect an *efficient resolution of problems in banks*. Where problems are remediable, supervisors will normally seek to identify and implement solutions that fully address their concerns; where they are not, the prompt and orderly exit of institutions that are no longer able to meet supervisory requirements is a necessary part of an efficient financial system. Forbearance, whether or not the result of political pressure, normally leads to worsening problems and higher resolution costs. The supervisory agency should be responsible for, or assist in, the orderly exit of problem banks in order to ensure that depositors are repaid to the fullest extent possible from the resources of the bank (supplemented by any applicable deposit insurance)[6] and ahead of shareholders, subordinated debt holders and other connected parties.

---

[6]As deposit insurance interacts with banking supervision, some basic principles are discussed in Appendix II.

In some cases, the best interests of depositors may be served by some form of restructuring, possibly takeover by a stronger institution or injection of new capital or shareholders. Supervisors may be able to facilitate such outcomes. It is essential that the end result fully meets all supervisory requirements, that it is realistically achievable in a short and determinate time frame, and that, in the interim, depositors are protected.

5. Deciding on the *appropriate level of systemic protection* is by and large a policy question to be taken by the relevant authorities (including the central bank), particularly where it may result in a commitment of public funds. Supervisors will also normally have a role to play because of their in-depth knowledge of the institutions involved. In order to preserve the operational independence of supervisors, it is important to draw a clear distinction between this systemic protection (or safety net) role and day-to-day supervision of solvent institutions. In handling systemic issues, it will be necessary to address, on the one hand, risks to confidence in the financial system and contagion to otherwise sound institutions, and, on the other hand, the need to minimise the distortion to market signals and discipline. Deposit insurance arrangements, where they exist, may also be triggered.

Principle 1. An effective system of banking supervision will have clear responsibilities and objectives for each agency involved in the supervision of banking organisations. Each such agency should possess operational independence and adequate resources. A suitable legal framework for banking supervision is also necessary, including provisions relating to authorisation of banking organisations and their ongoing supervision; powers to address compliance with laws as well as safety and soundness concerns; and legal protection for supervisors. Arrangements for sharing information between supervisors and protecting the confidentiality of such information should be in place.

This standard requires the following components to be in place:

- a clear, achievable and consistent framework of responsibilities and objectives set by legislation for (each of) the supervisor(s) involved, but with operational independence to pursue them free from political pressure and with accountability for achieving them;
- adequate resources (including staffing, funding and technology) to meet the objectives set, provided on terms that do not undermine the autonomy, integrity and independence of the supervisory agency;
- a framework of banking law that sets out minimum standards that banks must meet; allows supervisors sufficient flexibility to set prudential

rules administratively, where necessary, to achieve the objectives set as well as to utilise qualitative judgement; provides powers to gather and independently verify information; and gives supervisors power to enforce a range of penalties that may be applied when prudential requirements are not being met (including powers to remove individuals, invoke sanctions and revoke licences);

- protection (normally in law) from personal and institutional liability for supervisory actions taken in good faith in the course of performing supervisory duties; and
- a system of interagency cooperation and sharing of relevant information among the various official agencies, both domestic and foreign, responsible for the safety and soundness of the financial system; this cooperation should be supported by arrangements for protecting the confidentiality of supervisory information and ensuring that it is used only for purposes related to the effective supervision of the institutions concerned.

Section III: Licensing Process and Approval for Changes in Structure

Principle 2. The permissible activities of institutions that are licensed and subject to supervision as banks must be clearly defined, and the use of the word "bank" in names should be controlled as far as possible.

Principle 3. The licensing authority must have the right to set criteria and reject applications for establishments that do not meet the standards set. The licensing process, at a minimum, should consist of an assessment of the banking organisation's ownership structure, directors and senior management, its operating plan and internal controls, and its projected financial condition, including its capital base; where the proposed owner or parent organisation is a foreign bank, the prior consent of its home country supervisor should be obtained.

In order to facilitate a healthy financial system, and to define precisely the population of institutions to be supervised, the arrangements for licensing banking organisations and the scope of activities governed by licences should be clearly defined. In particular, at a minimum, the activity of taking a proper bank deposit from the public would typically be reserved for institutions that are licensed and subject to supervision as banks. The term "bank" should be clearly defined and the use of the word "bank"[7] in names should be controlled to the extent possible in those circumstances where the general public might be misled by unli-

---

[7]This includes any derivations of the word "bank," including "banking."

censed, unsupervised institutions implying otherwise by the use of "bank" in their titles.

By basing banking supervision on a system of licensing (or chartering) deposit-taking institutions (and, where appropriate, other types of financial institutions), the supervisors will have a means of identifying the population to be supervised and entry to the banking system will be controlled. The licensing authority should determine that new banking organisations have suitable shareholders, adequate financial strength, a legal structure in line with its operational structure, and management with sufficient expertise and integrity to operate the bank in a sound and prudent manner. It is important that the criteria for issuing licences are consistent with those applied in ongoing supervision so that they can provide one of the bases for withdrawing authorisation when an established institution no longer meets the criteria. Where the licensing and supervisory authorities are different, it is essential that they cooperate closely in the licensing process and that the supervisory authority has a legal right to have its views considered by the licensing authority. Clear and objective criteria also reduce the potential for political interference in the licensing process. Although the licensing process cannot guarantee that a bank will be well run after it opens, it can be an effective method for reducing the number of unstable institutions that enter the banking system. Licensing regulations, as well as supervisory tools, should be designed to limit the number of bank failures and the amount of depositor losses without inhibiting the efficiency and competitiveness of the banking industry by blocking entry to it. Both elements are necessary to maintain public confidence in the banking system.

Having established strict criteria for reviewing a banking licence application, the licensing authority must have the right to reject applications if it cannot be satisfied that the criteria set are met. The licensing process, at a minimum, should consist of an assessment of the banking organisation's ownership structure, directors and senior management, its operating plan and internal controls, and its projected financial condition, including its capital adequacy; when the proposed owner is a foreign bank, prior consent of its home country supervisor should be obtained.

A. Ownership Structure

Supervisors must be able to assess the ownership structure of banking organisations. This assessment should include the bank's direct and indirect controlling and major[8] direct or indirect shareholders. This assessment should review the controlling shareholders' past banking and non-banking business ventures and their integrity and standing in the business community, as well as the financial strength of all major shareholders and their ability to provide further financial support should it be needed. As part of the process of checking integrity and standing, the supervisor should determine the source of the initial capital to be invested.

Where a bank will be part of a larger organisation, licensing and supervisory authorities should determine that the ownership and organisational structure will not be a source of weakness and will minimise the risk to depositors of contagion from the activities conducted by other entities within the larger organisation. The other interests of the bank's major shareholders should be reviewed and the financial condition of these related entities assessed. The bank should not be used as a captive source of finance for its owners. When evaluating the corporate affiliations and structure of the proposed bank within a conglomerate, the licensing and supervisory authorities should determine that there will be sufficient transparency to permit them to identify the individuals responsible for the sound operations of the bank and to ensure that these individuals have the autonomy within the conglomerate structure to respond quickly to supervisory recommendations and requirements. Finally, the licensing and supervisory authorities must have the authority to prevent corporate affiliations or structures that hinder the effective supervision of banks. These can include structures where material parts are in jurisdictions where secrecy laws or inadequate financial supervision are significant obstacles and structures where the same owners control banks with parallel structures which cannot be subjected to consolidated supervision because there is no common corporate link.

B. Operating Plan, Systems of Control and Internal Organisation

Another element to review during the licensing process is the operations and strategies proposed for the bank. The operating plan should describe and analyse the market area from which the bank expects to draw the majority of its business and establish a strategy for the bank's ongoing operations. The application should also describe how the bank will be organised and controlled internally. The licensing agency should determine if these arrangements are consistent with the proposed strategy and should also determine whether adequate internal policies and procedures have been developed and adequate resources deployed. This should include determining that appropriate corporate governance will be in place (a management structure with clear accountability, a board of directors with ability to provide an independent check on management, and independent audit and compliance functions) and that the "four eyes" principle

---

[8]In many countries, a "major" shareholder is defined as holding 10% or more of a bank's equity capital.

(segregation of various functions, cross-checking, dual control of assets, double signatures, etc.) will be followed. It is essential to determine that the legal and operational structures will not inhibit supervision on either a solo or consolidated basis and that the supervisor will have adequate access to management and information. For this reason, supervisors should not grant a licence to a bank when the head office will be located outside its jurisdiction unless the supervisor is assured that it will have adequate access to management and information. (See Section E below for licensing of banks incorporated abroad.)

C. Fit and Proper Test for Directors and Senior Managers

A key aspect of the licensing process is an evaluation of the competence, integrity and qualifications of proposed management, including the board of directors.[9] The licensing agency should obtain the necessary information about the proposed directors and senior managers to consider individually and collectively their banking experience, other business experience, personal integrity and relevant skill. This evaluation of management should involve background checks on whether previous activities, including regulatory or judicial judgements, raise doubts concerning their competence, sound judgement, or honesty. It is critical that the bank's proposed management team includes a substantial number of individuals with a proven track record in banking. Supervisors should have the authority to require notification of subsequent changes in directors and senior management and to prevent such appointments if they are deemed to be detrimental to the interests of depositors.

D. Financial Projections Including Capital

The licensing agency should review pro forma financial statements and projections for the proposed bank. The review should determine whether the bank will have sufficient capital to support its proposed strategic plan, especially in light of start-up costs and possible operational losses in the early stages. In addition, the licensing authority should assess whether the projections are consistent and realistic, and whether the proposed bank is likely to be viable. In most countries, licensing agencies have established a minimum initial capital amount. The licensing agency should also consider the ability of shareholders to supply additional support, if needed, once the bank has com-

menced activities. If there will be a corporate shareholder with a significant holding, an assessment of the financial condition of the corporate parent should be made, including its capital strength.

E. Prior Approval from the Home Country Supervisor When the Proposed Owner Is a Foreign Bank (see also Section VI.B.)

When a foreign bank, subsidiary of a foreign banking group, or a foreign non-banking financial institution (subject to a supervisory authority) proposes to establish a local bank or branch office, the licensing authority should consider whether the Basle Minimum Standards[10] are met and in particular the licence should not normally be approved until the consent of the home country supervisor of the bank or banking group has been obtained. The host authority should also consider whether the home country supervisor capably performs its supervisory task on a consolidated basis.[11] In assessing whether capable consolidated supervision is provided, the host licensing authority should consider not only the nature and scope of the home country supervisory regime but also whether the structure of the applicant or its group is such as to not inhibit effective supervision by the home and host country supervisory authorities.

F. Transfer of a Bank's Shares

Principle 4. Banking supervisors must have the authority to review and reject any proposals to transfer significant ownership or controlling interests in existing banks to other parties.

In addition to licensing new banks, banking supervisors should be notified of any future significant direct or indirect investment in the bank or any increases or other changes in ownership over a particular threshold and should have the power to block such investments or prevent the exercise of voting rights in respect of such investments if they do not meet criteria comparable to those used for approving new banks. Notifications are often required for ownership or voting control involving established percentages of a bank's outstanding shares.[12] The threshold for approval of significant ownership changes may be higher than that for notification.

---

[9]With regard to the "fit and proper" evaluation, where appropriate, differentiation can be made between the supervisory board and the executive board.

[10]See "*Minimum standards for the supervision of international banking groups and their cross-border establishments*"—Volume III of the Compendium.

[11]See "*The supervision of cross-border banking*" (Annex B)—Volume III of the Compendium - for guidance on assessing whether a supervisor capably performs such tasks.

[12]These established percentages typically range between 5 and 10%.

G. Major Acquisitions or Investments by a Bank

Principle 5. Banking supervisors must have the authority to establish criteria for reviewing major acquisitions or investments by a bank and ensuring that corporate affiliations or structures do not expose the bank to undue risks or hinder effective supervision.

In many countries, once a bank has been licensed, it may conduct any activities normally permissible for banks or any range of activities specified in the banking licence. Consequently, certain acquisitions or investments may be automatically permissible if they comply with certain limits set by the supervisors or by banking law or regulation.

In certain circumstances, supervisors require banks to provide notice or obtain explicit permission before making certain acquisitions or investments. In these instances, supervisors need to determine if the banking organisation has both the financial and managerial resources to make the acquisition and may need to consider also whether the investment is permissible under existing banking laws and regulations. The supervisor should clearly define what types and amounts of investments need prior approval and for what cases notification is sufficient. Notification after the fact is most appropriate in those instances where the activity is closely related to banking and the investment is small relative to the bank's total capital.

Section IV: Arrangements for Ongoing Banking Supervision

A. Risks in Banking

Banking, by its nature, entails taking a wide array of risks. Banking supervisors need to understand these risks and be satisfied that banks are adequately measuring and managing them. The key risks faced by banks are discussed below.

Credit Risk

The extension of loans is the primary activity of most banks. Lending activities require banks to make judgements related to the creditworthiness of borrowers. These judgements do not always prove to be accurate and the creditworthiness of a borrower may decline over time due to various factors. Consequently, a major risk that banks face is credit risk or the failure of a counterparty to perform according to a contractual arrangement. This risk applies not only to loans but to other on- and off-balance sheet exposures such as guarantees, acceptances and securities investments. Serious banking problems have arisen from the failure of banks to recognise impaired assets, to create reserves for writing off these assets, and to suspend recognition of interest income when appropriate.

Large exposures to a single borrower, or to a group of related borrowers are a common cause of banking problems in that they represent a credit risk concentration. Large concentrations can also arise with respect to particular industries, economic sectors, or geographical regions or by having sets of loans with other characteristics that make them vulnerable to the same economic factors (e.g., highly leveraged transactions).

Connected lending—the extension of credit to individuals or firms connected to the bank through ownership or through the ability to exert direct or indirect control—if not properly controlled, can lead to significant problems because determinations regarding the creditworthiness of the borrower are not always made objectively. Connected parties include a bank's parent organisation, major shareholders, subsidiaries, affiliated entities, directors, and executive officers. Firms are also connected when they are controlled by the same family or group. In these, or in similar, circumstances, the connection can lead to preferential treatment in lending and thus greater risk of loan losses.

Country and Transfer Risk

In addition to the counterparty credit risk inherent in lending, international lending also includes country risk, which refers to risks associated with the economic, social and political environments of the borrower's home country. Country risk may be most apparent when lending to foreign governments or their agencies, since such lending is typically unsecured, but is important to consider when making any foreign loan or investment, whether to public or private borrowers. There is also a component of country risk called "transfer risk" which arises when a borrower's obligation is not denominated in the local currency. The currency of the obligation may become unavailable to the borrower regardless of its particular financial condition.

Market Risk

Banks face a risk of losses in on- and off-balance sheet positions arising from movements in market prices. Established accounting principles cause these risks to be typically most visible in a bank's trading activities, whether they involve debt or equity instruments, or foreign exchange or commodity positions. One specific element of market risk is foreign exchange risk. Banks act as "market-makers" in foreign exchange by quoting rates to their customers and by taking open positions in currencies. The risks inherent in foreign exchange business, particularly in running open foreign exchange positions, are increased during periods of instability in exchange rates.

Interest Rate Risk

Interest rate risk refers to the exposure of a bank's financial condition to adverse movements in interest rates. This risk impacts both the earnings of a bank and the economic value of its assets, liabilities and off-balance sheet instruments. The primary forms of interest rate risk to which banks are typically exposed are: (1) repricing risk, which arises from timing differences in the maturity (for fixed rate) and repricing (for floating rate) of bank assets, liabilities and off-balance sheet positions; (2) yield curve risk, which arises from changes in the slope and shape of the yield curve; (3) basis risk, which arises from imperfect correlation in the adjustment of the rates earned and paid on different instruments with otherwise similar repricing characteristics; and (4) optionality, which arises from the express or implied options imbedded in many bank assets, liabilities and off-balance sheet portfolios.

Although such risk is a normal part of banking, excessive interest rate risk can pose a significant threat to a bank's earnings and capital base. Managing this risk is of growing importance in sophisticated financial markets where customers actively manage their interest rate exposure. Special attention should be paid to this risk in countries where interest rates are being deregulated.

Liquidity Risk

Liquidity risk arises from the inability of a bank to accommodate decreases in liabilities or to fund increases in assets. When a bank has inadequate liquidity, it cannot obtain sufficient funds, either by increasing liabilities or by converting assets promptly, at a reasonable cost, thereby affecting profitability. In extreme cases, insufficient liquidity can lead to the insolvency of a bank.

Operational Risk

The most important types of operational risk involve breakdowns in internal controls and corporate governance. Such breakdowns can lead to financial losses through error, fraud, or failure to perform in a timely manner or cause the interests of the bank to be compromised in some other way, for example, by its dealers, lending officers or other staff exceeding their authority or conducting business in an unethical or risky manner. Other aspects of operational risk include major failure of information technology systems or events such as major fires or other disasters.

Legal Risk

Banks are subject to various forms of legal risk. This can include the risk that assets will turn out to be worth less or liabilities will turn out to be greater than expected because of inadequate or incorrect legal advice or documentation. In addition, existing laws may fail to resolve legal issues involving a bank; a court case involving a particular bank may have wider implications for banking business and involve costs to it and many or all other banks; and laws affecting banks or other commercial enterprises may change. Banks are particularly susceptible to legal risks when entering new types of transactions and when the legal right of a counterparty to enter into a transaction is not established.

Reputational Risk

Reputational risk arises from operational failures, failure to comply with relevant laws and regulations, or other sources. Reputational risk is particularly damaging for banks since the nature of their business requires maintaining the confidence of depositors, creditors and the general marketplace.

B. Development and Implementation of Prudential Regulations and Requirements

The risks inherent in banking must be recognised, monitored and controlled. Supervisors play a critical role in ensuring that bank management does this. An important part of the supervisory process is the authority of supervisors to develop and utilise prudential regulations and requirements to control these risks, including those covering capital adequacy, loan loss reserves, asset concentrations, liquidity, risk management and internal controls. These may be qualitative and/or quantitative requirements. Their purpose is to limit imprudent risk-taking by banks. These requirements should not supplant management decisions but rather impose minimum prudential standards to ensure that banks conduct their activities in an appropriate manner. The dynamic nature of banking requires that supervisors periodically assess their prudential requirements and evaluate the continued relevance of existing requirements as well as the need for new requirements.

1. Capital Adequacy

Principle 6. Banking supervisors must set prudent and appropriate minimum capital adequacy requirements for all banks. Such requirements should reflect the risks that the banks undertake, and must define the components of capital, bearing in mind their ability to absorb losses. At least for internationally active banks, these requirements must not be less than those established in the Basle Capital Accord and its amendments.

Equity capital serves several purposes: it provides a permanent source of revenue for the shareholders and funding for the bank; it is available to bear risk and absorb losses; it provides a base for further growth; and it gives the shareholders reason to ensure that the bank is managed in a safe and sound manner. Minimum capital adequacy ratios are necessary to reduce the risk of loss to depositors, creditors and other stakeholders of the bank and to help supervisors pursue the overall stability of the banking industry. Supervisors must set prudent and appropriate minimum capital adequacy requirements and encourage banks to operate with capital in excess of the minimum. Supervisors should consider requiring higher than minimum capital ratios when it appears appropriate due to the particular risk profile of the bank or if there are uncertainties regarding the asset quality, risk concentrations or other adverse characteristics of a bank's financial condition. If a bank's ratio falls below the minimum, banking supervisors should ensure that it has realistic plans to restore the minimum in a timely fashion. Supervisors should also consider whether additional restrictions are needed in such cases.

In 1988, the member countries of the Basle Committee on Banking Supervision agreed to a method of ensuring a bank's capital adequacy.[13] Many other countries have adopted the Capital Accord or something very close to it. The Accord addresses two important elements of a bank's activities: (1) different levels of credit risk inherent in its balance sheet and (2) off-balance sheet activities, which can represent a significant risk exposure.

The Accord defines what types of capital are acceptable for supervisory purposes and stresses the need for adequate levels of "core capital" (in the accord this capital is referred to as tier one capital) consisting of permanent shareholders' equity and disclosed reserves that are created or maintained by appropriations of retained earnings or other surplus (e.g., share premiums, retained profit, general reserves and reserves required by law). Disclosed reserves also include general funds that meet the following criteria: (1) allocations to the funds must be made out of post-tax retained earnings or out of pretax earnings adjusted for all potential tax liabilities; (2) the funds and movements into or out of them must be disclosed separately in the bank's published accounts; (3) the funds must be available to a bank to meet losses; and (4) losses cannot be charged directly to the funds but must be taken through the profit and loss account. The Accord also acknowledges other forms of supplementary capital (referred to as tier two capital), such as other forms of reserves and hybrid capital instruments that should be included within a system of capital measurement.

The Accord assigns risk weights to on- and off-balance sheet exposures according to broad categories of relative riskiness. The framework of weights has been kept as simple as possible with only five weights being used: 0, 10, 20, 50 and 100%.

The Accord sets minimum capital ratio requirements for internationally active banks of 4% tier one capital and 8% total (tier one plus tier two) capital in relation to risk-weighted assets.[14] These requirements are applied to banks on a consolidated basis.[15] It must be stressed that these ratios are considered a minimum standard and many supervisors require higher ratios or apply stricter definitions of capital or higher risk weights than set out in the Accord.

2. Credit Risk Management

(i) Credit-granting standards and credit monitoring process

Principle 7. An essential part of any supervisory system is the evaluation of a bank's policies, practices and procedures related to the granting of loans and making of investments and the ongoing management of the loan and investment portfolios.

Supervisors need to ensure that the credit and investment function at individual banks is objective and grounded in sound principles. The maintenance of prudent written lending policies, loan approval and administration procedures, and appropriate loan documentation are essential to a bank's management of the lending function. Lending and investment activities should be based on prudent underwriting standards that are approved by the bank's board of directors and clearly communicated to the bank's lending officers and staff. It is also critical for supervisors to determine the extent to which the institution makes its credit decisions free of conflicting interests and inappropriate pressure from outside parties.

Banks must also have a well-developed process for ongoing monitoring of credit relationships, including the financial condition of borrowers. A key element of any management information system should be a data base that provides essential details on the condition of the loan portfolio, including internal loan grading and classifications.

(ii) Assessment of asset quality and adequacy of loan loss provisions and reserves

Principle 8. Banking supervisors must be satisfied that banks establish and adhere to adequate policies, practices and procedures for evaluating the quality of assets and the adequacy of loan loss provisions and loan loss reserves.

---

[13]See "*International convergence of capital measurement and capital standards*"—Volume I of the Compendium.

[14]Although the Accord applies to internationally active banks, many countries also apply the Accord to their domestic banks.

[15]Supervisors should, of course, also give consideration to monitoring the capital adequacy of banks on a non-consolidated basis.

Supervisors should assess a bank's policies regarding the periodic review of individual credits, asset classification and provisioning. They should be satisfied that these policies are being reviewed regularly and implemented consistently. Supervisors should also ensure that banks have a process in place for overseeing problem credits and collecting past due loans. When the level of problem credits at a bank is of concern to the supervisors, they should require the bank to strengthen its lending practices, credit-granting standards, and overall financial strength.

When guarantees or collateral are provided, the bank should have a mechanism in place for continually assessing the strength of these guarantees and appraising the worth of the collateral. Supervisors should also ensure that banks properly record and hold adequate capital against off-balance sheet exposures when they retain contingent risks.

(iii) Concentrations of risk and large exposures

Principle 9. Banking supervisors must be satisfied that banks have management information systems that enable management to identify concentrations within the portfolio and supervisors must set prudential limits to restrict bank exposures to single borrowers or groups of related borrowers.

Banking supervisors must set prudential limits to restrict bank exposures to single borrowers, groups of related borrowers and other significant risk concentrations.[16] These limits are usually expressed in terms of a percentage of bank capital and, although they vary, 25% of capital is typically the most that a bank or banking group may extend to a private sector non-bank borrower or a group of closely related borrowers without specific supervisory approval. It is recognised that newly established or very small banks may face practical limits on their ability to diversify, necessitating higher levels of capital to reflect the resultant risk.

Supervisors should monitor the bank's handling of concentrations of risk and may require that banks report to them any such exposures exceeding a specified limit (e.g., 10% of capital) or exposures to large borrowers as determined by the supervisors. In some countries, the aggregate of such large exposures is also subject to limits.

(iv) Connected lending

---

[16] As a guide to appropriate controls on concentrations of risk, the Basle Committee has adopted a best practices paper covering large credit exposures. This 1991 paper addresses the definitions of credit exposures, single borrowers, and related counterparties, and also discusses appropriate levels of large exposure limits, and risks arising from different forms of asset concentrations. See *"Measuring and controlling large credit exposures"*—Volume I of the Compendium.

Principle 10. In order to prevent abuses arising from connected lending, banking supervisors must have in place requirements that banks lend to related companies and individuals on an arm's-length basis, that such extensions of credit are effectively monitored, and that other appropriate steps are taken to control or mitigate the risks.

Banking supervisors must be able to prevent abuses arising from connected and related party lending. This will require ensuring that such lending is conducted only on an arm's-length basis and that the amount of credit extended is monitored. These controls are most easily implemented by requiring that the terms and conditions of such credits not be more favourable than credit extended to non-related borrowers under similar circumstances and by imposing strict limits on such lending. Supervisors should have the authority, in appropriate circumstances, to go further and establish absolute limits on categories of such loans, to deduct such lending from capital when assessing capital adequacy, or to require collateralisation of such loans. Transactions with related parties that pose special risks to the bank should be subject to the approval of the bank's board of directors, reported to the supervisors, or prohibited altogether. Supervising banking organisations on a consolidated basis can in some circumstances identify and reduce problems arising from connected lending.

Supervisors should also have the authority to make discretionary judgements about the existence of connections between the bank and other parties. This is especially necessary in those instances where the bank and related parties have taken measures to conceal such connections.

(v) Country and transfer risk

Principle 11. Banking supervisors must be satisfied that banks have adequate policies and procedures for identifying, monitoring and controlling country risk and transfer risk in their international lending and investment activities, and for maintaining appropriate reserves against such risks.[17]

3. Market Risk Management

Principle 12. Banking supervisors must be satisfied that banks have in place systems that accurately measure, monitor and adequately control market risks; supervisors should have powers to impose specific limits and/or a specific capital charge on market risk exposures, if warranted.

---

[17] These issues were addressed in a 1982 Basle Committee paper *"Management of banks' international lending"*—Volume I of the Compendium.

Banking supervisors must determine that banks accurately measure and adequately control market risks. Where material, it is appropriate to provide an explicit capital cushion for the price risks to which banks are exposed, particularly those arising from their trading activities. Introducing the discipline that capital requirements impose can be an important further step in strengthening the soundness and stability of financial markets. There should also be well-structured quantitative and qualitative standards for the risk management process related to market risk.[18] Banking supervisors should also ensure that bank management has set appropriate limits and implemented adequate internal controls for their foreign exchange business.[19]

4. Other Risk Management

Principle 13. Banking supervisors must be satisfied that banks have in place a comprehensive risk management process (including appropriate board and senior management oversight) to identify, measure, monitor and control all other material risks and, where appropriate, to hold capital against these risks.

Risk management standards[20] are a necessary element of banking supervision, and increasingly important as financial instruments and risk measurement techniques become more complex. Moreover, the effect of new technologies on financial markets both permits and requires many banks to monitor their portfolios daily and adjust risk exposures rapidly in response to market and customer needs. In this environment, management, investors, and supervisors need information about a bank's exposures that is correct, informative, and provided on a timely basis. Supervisors can contribute to this process by promoting and enforcing sound policies in banks, and requiring

procedures that ensure the necessary information is available.

(i) Interest rate risk

Supervisors should monitor the way in which banks control interest rate risk including effective board and senior management oversight, adequate risk management policies and procedures, risk measurement and monitoring systems, and comprehensive controls.[21] In addition, supervisors should receive sufficient and timely information from banks in order to evaluate the level of interest rate risk. This information should take appropriate account of the range of maturities and currencies in each bank's portfolio, as well as other relevant factors such as the distinction between trading and non-trading activities.

(ii) Liquidity management

The purpose of liquidity management is to ensure that the bank is able to meet fully its contractual commitments. Crucial elements of strong liquidity management include good management information systems, central liquidity control, analysis of net funding requirements under alternative scenarios, diversification of funding sources, and contingency planning.[22] Supervisors should expect banks to manage their assets, liabilities and off-balance sheet contracts with a view to maintaining adequate liquidity. Banks should have a diversified funding base, both in terms of sources of funds and the maturity breakdown of the liabilities. They should also maintain an adequate level of liquid assets.

(iii) Operational risk

Supervisors should ensure that senior management puts in place effective internal control and auditing procedures; also, that they have policies for managing or mitigating operational risk (e.g., through insurance or contingency planning). Supervisors should determine that banks have adequate and well-tested business resumption plans for all major systems, with remote site facilities, to protect against such events.

---

[18]In January 1996 the Basle Committee issued a paper amending the Capital Accord and implementing a new capital charge related to market risk. This capital charge comes into effect by the end of 1997. In calculating the capital charge, banks will have the option of using a standardised method or their own internal models. The G-10 supervisory authorities plan to use "backtesting" (i.e., ex-post comparisons between model results and actual performance) in conjunction with banks' internal risk measurement systems as a basis for applying capital charges. See "*Overview of the Amendment to the Capital Accord to incorporate market risks,*" "*Amendment to the Capital Accord to incorporate market risks,*" and "*Supervisory framework for the use of 'backtesting' in conjunction with the internal models approach to market risk capital requirements*"—Volume II of the Compendium.

[19]See "*Supervision of banks' foreign exchange positions*"—Volume I of the Compendium.

[20]The Basle Committee has recently established a sub-group to study issues related to risk management and internal controls and to provide guidance to the banking industry.

[21] The Basle Committee has recently issued a paper related to the management of interest rate risk that outlines a number of principles for use by supervisory authorities when considering interest rate risk management at individual banks. See "*Principles for the management of interest rate risk*"—Volume I of the Compendium.

[22]The Basle Committee has issued a paper that sets out the main elements of a model analytical framework for measuring and managing liquidity. Although the paper focuses on the use of the framework by large, internationally active banks, it provides guidance that should prove useful to all banks. See "*A framework for measuring and managing liquidity*"—Volume I of the Compendium.

5. Internal Controls

Principle 14. Banking supervisors must determine that banks have in place internal controls that are adequate for the nature and scale of their business. These should include clear arrangements for delegating authority and responsibility; separation of the functions that involve committing the bank, paying away its funds, and accounting for its assets and liabilities; reconciliation of these processes; safeguarding its assets; and appropriate independent internal or external audit and compliance functions to test adherence to these controls as well as applicable laws and regulations.

Principle 15. Banking supervisors must determine that banks have adequate policies, practices and procedures in place, including strict "know-your-customer" rules, that promote high ethical and professional standards in the financial sector and prevent the bank being used, intentionally or unintentionally, by criminal elements.

The purpose of internal controls is to ensure that the business of a bank is conducted in a prudent manner in accordance with policies and strategies established by the bank's board of directors; that transactions are only entered into with appropriate authority; that assets are safeguarded and liabilities controlled; that accounting and other records provide complete, accurate and timely information; and that management is able to identify, assess, manage and control the risks of the business.

There are four primary areas of internal controls:

- organisational structures (definitions of duties and responsibilities, discretionary limits for loan approval, and decision-making procedures);
- accounting procedures (reconciliation of accounts, control lists, periodic trial balances, etc.);
- the "four eyes" principle (segregation of various functions, cross-checking, dual control of assets, double signatures, etc.); and
- physical control over assets and investments.

These controls must be supplemented by an effective audit function that independently evaluates the adequacy, operational effectiveness and efficiency of the control systems within an organisation. Consequently, the internal auditor must have an appropriate status within the bank and adequate reporting lines designed to safeguard his or her independence.[23] The external audit can provide a cross-check on the effectiveness of this process. Banking supervisors must be satisfied that effective policies and practices are followed and that management takes appropriate corrective action in response to internal control weaknesses identified by internal and external auditors.

Banks are subject to a wide array of banking and non-banking laws and regulations and must have in place adequate policies and procedures to ensure compliance. Otherwise, violations of established requirements can damage the reputation of the bank and expose it to penalties. In extreme cases, this damage could threaten the bank's solvency. Compliance failures also indicate that the bank is not being managed with the integrity and skill expected of a banking organisation. Larger banks in particular should have independent compliance functions and banking supervisors should determine that such functions are operating effectively.

Public confidence in banks can be undermined, and bank reputations damaged, as a result of association (even if inadvertent) with drug traders and other criminals. Consequently, while banking supervisors are not generally responsible for the criminal prosecution of money laundering offences or the ongoing anti-money laundering efforts in their countries, they have a role in ensuring that banks have procedures in place, including strict "know-your-customer" policies, to avoid association or involvement with drug traders and other criminals, as well as in the general promotion of high ethical and professional standards in the financial sector.[24] Specifically, supervisors should encourage the adoption of those recommendations of the Financial Action Task Force on Money Laundering (FATF) that apply to financial institutions. These relate to customer identification and record-keeping, increased diligence by financial institutions in detecting and reporting suspicious transactions, and measures to deal with countries with insufficient or no anti-money laundering measures.

The occurrence of fraud in banks, or involving them, is also of concern to banking supervisors for three reasons. On a large scale it may threaten the solvency of banks and the integrity and soundness of the financial system. Second, it may be indicative of weak internal controls that will require supervisory attention. And thirdly, there are potential reputational and confidence implications which may also spread from a particular institution to the system. For these reasons, banks should have established lines of communication, both within the management chain and within an internal security or guardian function independent of management, for reporting problems. Employees should be required to report suspicious or troubling behaviour to a superior or to internal security. Moreover, banks should be required to report suspicious activities and significant incidents of fraud to

---

[23]In some countries, supervisors recommend that banks establish an "audit committee" within the board of directors. The purpose of this committee is to facilitate the effective performance of board oversight.

[24]See *"Prevention of criminal use of the banking system for the purpose of money-laundering"*—Volume I of the Compendium.

the supervisors. It is not necessarily the role of supervisors to investigate fraud in banks, and the skills required to do so are specialised, but supervisors do need to ensure that appropriate authorities have been alerted. They need to be able to consider and, if necessary, act to prevent effects on other banks and to maintain an awareness of the types of fraudulent activity that are being undertaken or attempted in order to ensure that banks have controls capable of countering them.

C. Methods of Ongoing Banking Supervision

Principle 16. An effective banking supervisory system should consist of some form of both on-site and off-site supervision.

Principle 17. Banking supervisors must have regular contact with bank management and a thorough understanding of the institution's operations.

Principle 18. Banking supervisors must have a means of collecting, reviewing and analysing prudential reports and statistical returns from banks on a solo and consolidated basis.

Principle 19. Banking supervisors must have a means of independent validation of supervisory information either through on-site examinations or use of external auditors.

Principle 20. An essential element of banking supervision is the ability of the supervisors to supervise the banking group on a consolidated basis.

Supervision requires the collection and analysis of information. This can be done on- or off-site. An effective supervisory system will use both means. In some countries, on-site work is carried out by examiners and in others by qualified external auditors. In still other countries, a mixed system of on-site examinations and collaboration between the supervisors and the external auditors exists. The extent of on-site work and the method by which it is carried out depend on a variety of factors.

Regardless of their mix of on-site and off-site activities or their use of work done by external accountants, banking supervisors must have regular contact with bank management and a thorough understanding of the institution's operations. Review of the reports of internal and external auditors can be an integral part of both on-site and off-site supervision. The various factors considered during the licensing process should be periodically assessed as part of ongoing supervision. Banks should be required to submit information on a periodic basis for review by the supervisors, and supervisors should be able to discuss regularly with banks all significant issues and areas of their business. If problems develop, banks should also feel that they can confide in and consult with the supervisor, and ex-

pect that problems will be discussed constructively and treated in a confidential manner. They must also recognise their responsibility to inform supervisors of important matters in a timely manner.

1. Off-Site Surveillance

Supervisors must have a means of collecting, reviewing and analysing prudential reports and statistical returns from banks on a solo and consolidated basis. These should include basic financial statements as well as supporting schedules that provide greater detail on exposure to different types of risk and various other financial aspects of the bank, including provisions and off-balance sheet activities. The supervisory agency should also have the ability to obtain information on affiliated non-bank entities. Banking supervisors should also make full use of publicly available information and analysis.

These reports can be used to check adherence to prudential requirements, such as capital adequacy or single debtor limits. Off-site monitoring can often identify potential problems, particularly in the interval between on-site inspections, thereby providing early detection and prompting corrective action before problems become more serious. Such reports can also be used to identify trends not only for particular institutions, but also for the banking system as a whole. These reports can provide the basis for discussions with bank management, either at periodic intervals or when problems appear. They should also be a key component of examination planning so that maximum benefit is achieved from the limited time spent conducting an on-site review.

2. On-Site Examination and/or Use of External Auditors[25]

Supervisors must have a means of validating supervisory information either through on-site examinations or use of external auditors. On-site work, whether done by examination staff of the banking supervisory agency or commissioned by supervisors but undertaken by external auditors, should be structured to provide independent verification that adequate corporate governance exists at individual banks and that information provided by banks is reliable.

On-site examinations provide the supervisor with a means of verifying or assessing a range of matters including:

- the accuracy of reports received from the bank;
- the overall operations and condition of the bank;

---

[25]In some countries, external auditors hired by the supervisory agency to conduct work on its behalf are referred to as reporting accountants.

- the adequacy of the bank's risk management systems and internal control procedures;
- the quality of the loan portfolio and adequacy of loan loss provisions and reserves;
- the competence of management;
- the adequacy of accounting and management information systems;
- issues identified in off-site or previous on-site supervisory processes;
- bank adherence to laws and regulations and the terms stipulated in the banking licence.

The supervisory agency should establish clear internal guidelines related to the frequency and scope of examinations. In addition, examination policies and procedures should be developed in order to ensure that examinations are conducted in a thorough and consistent manner with clear objectives.

Depending on its use of examination staff, a supervisory agency may use external auditors to fulfil the above functions in whole or in part. In some cases, such functions may be part of the normal audit process (e.g., assessing the quality of the loan portfolio and the level of provisions that need to be held against it). In other areas, the supervisor should have adequate powers to require work to be commissioned specifically for supervisory purposes (e.g., on the accuracy of reports filed with supervisors or the adequacy of control systems). However, the work of external auditors should be utilised for supervisory purposes only when there is a well-developed, professionally independent auditing profession with skills to undertake the work required. In these circumstances, the supervisory agency needs to reserve the right to veto the appointment of a particular firm of external auditors where supervisory reliance is to be placed on the firm's work. In addition, supervisors should urge banking groups to use common auditors and common accounting dates throughout the group, to the extent possible.

It is also important that the supervisors and external auditors have a clear understanding of their respective roles. Before problems are detected at a bank, the external auditors should clearly understand their responsibilities for communicating with the supervisory agency and should also be protected from personal liability for disclosures, in good faith, of such information. A mechanism should be in place to facilitate discussions between the supervisors and external auditors.[26] In many instances, these discussions should also include the bank.

In all cases, the supervisory agency should have the legal authority and means to conduct independent checks of banks based on identified concerns.

3. Supervision on a Consolidated Basis

An essential element of banking supervision is the ability of the supervisors to supervise the consolidated banking organisation. This includes the ability to review both banking and non-banking activities conducted by the banking organisation, either directly or indirectly (through subsidiaries and affiliates), and activities conducted at both domestic and foreign offices. Supervisors need to take into account that non-financial activities of a bank or group may pose risks to the bank. Supervisors should decide which prudential requirements will be applied on a bank-only (solo) basis, which ones will be applied on a consolidated basis, and which ones will be applied on both bases. In all cases, the banking supervisors should be aware of the overall structure of the banking organisation or group when applying their supervisory methods.[27] Banking supervisors should also have the ability to coordinate with other authorities responsible for supervising specific entities within the organisation's structure.

D. Information Requirements of Banking Organisations

Principle 21. Banking supervisors must be satisfied that each bank maintains adequate records drawn up in accordance with consistent accounting policies and practices that enable the supervisor to obtain a true and fair view of the financial condition of the bank and the profitability of its business, and that the bank publishes on a regular basis financial statements that fairly reflect its condition.

For banking supervisors to conduct effective off-site supervision of banks and to evaluate the condition of the local banking market, they must receive financial information at regular intervals and this information must be verified periodically through on-site examinations or external audits. Banking supervisors must ensure that each bank maintains adequate accounting records drawn up in accordance with consistent accounting policies and practices that enable the supervisor to obtain a true and fair view of the financial condition of the bank and the profitability of its business. In order that the accounts portray a true and fair view, it is essential that assets are recorded at values that are realistic and consistent, taking account of current values, where relevant, and that profit reflects what, on a net basis, is likely to be received and takes

---

[26] The Basle Committee has reviewed the relationship between bank supervisors and external auditors and has developed best practices for supervisors with regard to their interaction with external auditors. See *"The relationship between bank supervisors and external auditors"*—Volume III of the Compendium.

[27] The Basle Committee recommended supervision on a consolidated basis in its paper *"Consolidated supervision of banks' international activities"*—Volume I of the Compendium.

into account likely transfers to loan loss reserves. It is important that banks submit information in a format that makes comparisons among banks possible although, for certain purposes, data derived from internal management information systems may also be helpful to supervisors. At a minimum, periodic reporting should include a bank's balance sheet, contingent liabilities and income statement, with supporting details and key risk exposures.

Supervisors can be obstructed or misled when banks knowingly or recklessly provide false information of material importance to the supervisory process. If a bank provides information to the supervisor knowing that it is materially false or misleading, or it does so recklessly, supervisory and/or criminal action should be taken against both the individuals involved and the institution.

1. Accounting Standards

In order to ensure that the information submitted by banks is of a comparable nature and its meaning is clear, the supervisory agency will need to provide report instructions that clearly establish the accounting standards to be used in preparing the reports. These standards should be based on accounting principles and rules that command wide international acceptance and be aimed specifically at banking institutions.

2. Scope and Frequency of Reporting

The supervisory agency needs to have powers to determine the scope and frequency of reporting to reflect the volatility of the business and to enable the agency to track what is happening at individual banks on both a solo and consolidated basis, as well as with the banking system as a whole. The supervisors should develop a series of informational reports for banks to prepare and submit at regular intervals. While some reports may be filed as often as monthly, others may be filed quarterly or annually. In addition, some reports may be "event generated," meaning they are filed only if a particular event occurs (e.g. investment in a new affiliate). Supervisors should be sensitive to the burden that reporting imposes. Consequently, they may determine that it is not necessary for every bank to file every report. Filing status can be based on the organisational structure of the bank, its size, and the types of activities it conducts.

3. Confirmation of the Accuracy of Information Submitted

It is the responsibility of bank management to ensure the accuracy, completeness and timeliness of prudential, financial, and other reports submitted to the supervisors. Therefore, bank management must en-

sure that reports are verified and that external auditors determine that the reporting systems in place are adequate and provide reliable data. External auditors should express an opinion on the annual accounts and management report supplied to shareholders and the general public. Weaknesses in bank auditing standards in a particular country may require that banking supervisors become involved in establishing clear guidelines concerning the scope and content of the audit programme as well as the standards to be used. In extreme cases where supervisors cannot be satisfied with the quality of the annual accounts or regulatory reports, or with the work done by external auditors, they should have the ability to use supervisory measures to bring about timely corrective action, and they may need to reserve the right to approve the issue of accounts to the public.

In assessing the nature and adequacy of work done by auditors, and the degree of reliance that can be placed on this work, supervisors will need to consider the extent to which the audit programme has examined such areas as the loan portfolio, loan loss reserves, non-performing assets (including the treatment of interest on such assets), asset valuations, trading and other securities activities, derivatives, asset securitisations, and the adequacy of internal controls over financial reporting. Where it is competent and independent of management, internal audits can be relied upon as a source of information and may contribute usefully to the supervisors' understanding.

4. Confidentiality of Supervisory Information

Although market participants should have access to correct and timely information, there are certain types of sensitive information[28] that should be held confidential by banking supervisors. In order for a relationship of mutual trust to develop, banks need to know that such sensitive information will be held confidential by the banking supervisory agency and its appropriate counterparts at other domestic and foreign supervisory agencies.

5. Disclosure

In order for market forces to work effectively, thereby fostering a stable and efficient financial system, market participants need access to correct and timely information. Disclosure, therefore, is a complement to supervision. For this reason, banks should be required to disclose to the public information regarding their activities and financial position that is com-

---

[28]The types of information considered sensitive vary from country to country; however, this typically includes information related to individual customer accounts as well as problems that the supervisor is helping the bank to resolve.

prehensive and not misleading. This information should be timely and sufficient for market participants to assess the risk inherent in any individual banking organisation.[29]

Section V: Formal Powers of Supervisors

Principle 22. Banking supervisors must have at their disposal adequate supervisory measures to bring about timely corrective action when banks fail to meet prudential requirements (such as minimum capital adequacy ratios), when there are regulatory violations, or where depositors are threatened in any other way. In extreme circumstances, this should include the ability to revoke the banking licence or recommend its revocation.

A. Corrective Measures

Despite the efforts of supervisors, situations can occur where banks fail to meet supervisory requirements or where their solvency comes into question. In order to protect depositors and creditors, and prevent more widespread contagion of such problems, supervisors must be able to conduct appropriate intervention. Banking supervisors must have at their disposal adequate supervisory measures to bring about timely corrective action and which enable a graduated response by supervisors depending on the nature of the problems detected. In those instances where the detected problem is relatively minor, informal action such as a simple oral or written communication to bank management may be all that is warranted. In other instances, more formal action may be necessary. These remedial measures have the greatest chance of success when they are part of a comprehensive programme of corrective action developed by the bank and with an implementation timetable; however, failure to achieve agreement with bank management should not inhibit the supervisory authority from requiring the necessary corrective action.

Supervisors should have the authority not only to restrict the current activities of the bank but also withhold approval for new activities or acquisitions. They should also have the authority to restrict or suspend dividend or other payments to shareholders, as well as to restrict asset transfers and a bank's purchase of its own shares. The supervisor should have effective means to address management problems, including the power to have controlling owners, directors, and managers replaced or their powers re-

stricted, and, where appropriate, barring individuals from the business of banking. In extreme cases, the supervisors should have the ability to impose conservatorship over a bank that is failing to meet prudential or other requirements. It is important that all remedial actions be addressed directly to the bank's board of directors since they have overall responsibility for the institution.

Once action has been taken or remedial measures have been imposed, supervisors must be vigilant in their oversight of the problems giving rise to it by periodically checking to determine that the bank is complying with the measures. There should be a progressive escalation of action or remedial measures if the problems become worse or if bank management ignores more informal requests from supervisors to take corrective action.

B. Liquidation Procedures

In the most extreme cases, and despite ongoing attempts by the supervisors to ensure that a problem situation is resolved, a banking organisation may no longer be financially viable. In such cases, the supervisor can be involved in resolutions that require a take-over by or merger with a healthier institution. When all other measures fail, the supervisor should have the ability to close or assist in the closing of an unhealthy bank in order to protect the overall stability of the banking system.

Section VI: Cross-Border Banking

The Principles set out in this section are consistent with the so-called Basle Concordat and its successors.[30] The Concordat establishes understandings relating to contact and collaboration between home and host country authorities in the supervision of banks' cross-border establishments. The most recent of these documents, *"The supervision of cross-border banking,"* was developed by the Basle Committee in collaboration with the Offshore Group of Banking Supervisors and subsequently endorsed by 130 countries attending the International Conference of Banking Supervisors in June 1996. This document contains twenty-nine recommendations aimed at removing obstacles to the implementation of effective consolidated supervision.

---

[29]The Basle Committee has recently established a sub-group to study issues related to disclosure and to provide guidance to the banking industry.

[30]See *"Principles for the supervision of banks' foreign establishments," "Minimum standards for the supervision of international banking groups and their cross-border establishments,"* and *"The supervision of cross-border banking,"* all contained in Volume III of the Compendium.

A. Obligations of Home Country Supervisors

Principle 23. Banking supervisors must practise global consolidated supervision over their internationally active banking organisations, adequately monitoring and applying appropriate prudential norms to all aspects of the business conducted by these banking organisations worldwide, primarily at their foreign branches, joint ventures and subsidiaries.

Principle 24. A key component of consolidated supervision is establishing contact and information exchange with the various other supervisors involved, primarily host country supervisory authorities.

As part of practising consolidated banking supervision, banking supervisors must adequately monitor and apply appropriate prudential norms to all aspects of the business conducted by their banking organisations worldwide including at their foreign branches, joint ventures and subsidiaries. A major responsibility of the parent bank supervisor is to determine that the parent bank is providing adequate oversight not only of its overseas branches but also its joint ventures and subsidiaries. This parent bank oversight should include monitoring compliance with internal controls, receiving an adequate and regular flow of information, and periodically verifying the information received. In many instances, a bank's foreign offices may be conducting business fundamentally different from the bank's domestic operations. Consequently, supervisors should determine that the bank has the expertise needed to conduct these activities in a safe and sound manner.

A key component of consolidated supervision is establishing contact and information exchange with the various other supervisors involved, including host country supervisory authorities. This contact should commence at the authorisation stage when the host supervisor should seek the approval from the home supervisor before issuing a licence. In many cases, bilateral arrangements exist between supervisors. These arrangements can prove helpful in defining the scope of information to be shared and the conditions under which such sharing would normally be expected. Unless satisfactory arrangements for obtaining information can be agreed, banking supervisors should prohibit their banks from establishing operations in countries with secrecy laws or other regulations prohibiting flows of information deemed necessary for adequate supervision.

The parent supervisor should also determine the nature and extent of supervision conducted by the host country of the local operations of the home country's banks. Where host country supervision is inadequate, the parent supervisor may need to take special additional measures to compensate, such as through on-site examinations, or by requiring additional information from the bank's head office or its external auditors. If these options cannot be developed to give sufficient comfort, bearing in mind the risks involved, then the home supervisor may have no option but to request the closure of the relevant overseas establishment.

B. Obligations of Host Country Supervisors

Principle 25. Banking supervisors must require the local operations of foreign banks to be conducted to the same high standards as are required of domestic institutions and must have powers to share information needed by the home country supervisors of those banks for the purpose of carrying out consolidated supervision.

Foreign banks often provide depth and increase competition and are therefore important participants in local banking markets. Banking supervisors must require the local operations of foreign banks to be conducted to the same high standards as are required of domestic institutions and must have powers to share information needed by the home country supervisors of those banks for the purpose of carrying out consolidated supervision. Consequently, foreign bank operations should be subject to similar prudential, inspection and reporting requirements as domestic banks (recognising, of course, obvious differences such as branches not being separately capitalised).

As the host country supervisory agency supervises only a limited part of the overall operations of the foreign bank, the supervisory agency should determine that the home country supervisor practices consolidated supervision of both the domestic and overseas operations of the bank. In order for home country supervisors to practice effectively consolidated supervision, the host country supervisor must share information about the local operations of foreign banks with them provided there is reciprocity and protection of the confidentiality of the information. In addition, home country supervisors should be given on-site access to local offices and subsidiaries for appropriate supervisory purposes. Where host country laws pose obstacles to sharing information or cooperating with home country supervisors, host authorities should work to have their laws changed in order to permit effective consolidated supervision by home countries.

APPENDIX I

Special Issues Related to Government-Owned Banks

Many countries have some commercial banks that are owned, wholly or substantially, by the national government or by other public bodies.[31] In other countries, government-owned commercial banks comprise the majority of the banking system, usually for historic reasons. In principle, all banks should be subject to the same operational and supervisory standards regardless of their ownership; however, the unique nature of government-owned commercial banks should be recognised.

Government-owned commercial banks typically are backed by the full resources of the government. This provides additional support and strength for these banks. Although this government support can be advantageous, it should also be noted that the correction of problems at these banks is sometimes deferred and the government is not always in a position to recapitalise the bank when required. At the same time, this support may lead to the taking of excessive risks by bank management. In addition, market discipline may be less effective when market participants know that a particular bank has the full backing of the government and consequently has access to more extensive (and possibly cheaper) funding than would be the case for a comparable privately owned bank.

Consequently, it is important that supervisors seek to ensure that government-owned commercial banks operate to the same high level of professional skill and disciplines as required of privately-owned commercial banks in order to preserve a strong credit and control culture in the banking system as a whole. In addition, supervisors should apply their supervisory methods in the same manner to government-owned commercial banks as they do to all other commercial banks.

---

[31]This can include savings banks and cooperative banks. These banks are different, however, from "policy" banks that typically specialise in certain types of lending or target certain sectors of the economy.

APPENDIX II

Deposit Protection

Despite the efforts of supervisors, bank failures can occur. At such times, the possible loss of all or part of their funds increases the risk that depositors will lose confidence in other banks. Consequently, many countries have established deposit insurance plans to protect small depositors. These plans are normally organised by the government or central bank, or by the relevant bankers' association and are compulsory rather than voluntary. Deposit insurance provides a safety net for many bank creditors thereby increasing public confidence in banks and making the financial system more stable. A safety net may also limit the effect that problems at one bank might have on other, healthier, banks in the same market, thereby reducing the possibility of contagion or a chain reaction within the banking system as a whole. A key benefit of deposit insurance is that, in conjunction with logical exit procedures, it gives the banking supervisors greater freedom to let problem banks fail.

Deposit insurance can however increase the risk of imprudent behaviour by individual banks. Small depositors will be less inclined to withdraw funds even if the bank pursues high-risk strategies, thus weakening an important check on imprudent management. Government officials and supervisors need to recognise this effect of a safety net and take steps to prevent excessive risk-taking by banks. One method of limiting risk-taking is to utilise a deposit insurance system consisting of "co-insurance." Under such a system, the deposit insurance covers a percentage (e.g., 90%) of individual deposits and/or provides cover only up to a certain absolute amount so that depositors still have some funds at risk. Other methods include charging risk-based premiums or withholding deposit insurance from large, institutional depositors.

The actual form of such a programme should be tailored to the circumstances in, as well as historical and cultural features of, each country.[32]

---

[32]Some form of banking deposit insurance exists in all of the member countries of the Basle Committee. The experiences of these countries should prove useful in designing a deposit insurance programme. See *Deposit protection schemes in the G-10 countries*—Volume III of the Compendium.

Annex II

IOSCO Principles and Recommendations for the Regulation and Supervision of Securities Markets

I. IOSCO: Structure and Objectives

IOSCO is the international forum for securities regulators, constituted by 134 member agencies from 81 countries. IOSCO's membership encompasses the whole range of agencies, associations and organizations involved in the regulation and development of securities markets world-wide. IOSCO's work program therefore has a global reach and global impact, both in terms of geography and range of affected markets.

As stated in the Organization's By-Laws, IOSCO members have resolved to:

- cooperate together to promote high standards of regulation in order to maintain just, efficient and sound markets;
- exchange information on their respective experiences in order to promote the development of domestic markets;
- unite their efforts to establish standards and an effective surveillance of international securities transactions;
- provide mutual assistance to promote the integrity of the markets by a rigorous application of the standards and by effective enforcement against offences.

Any agency requesting admission to the membership of IOSCO must commit to these basic principles as well as to the Resolutions adopted by IOSCO's Presidents Committee before the application is considered.

II. The Work of IOSCO: Consensus and Cooperation

IOSCO's work program is designed to develop high-quality standards and promote market integrity through a process of member consensus and cooperation. Management of the Organization is the responsibility of the Executive Committee, an elected body consisting of 19 member agencies. The substantive work of the Organization is conducted by the Technical Committee and the Emerging Markets Committee

("EMC"), with important policy and organizational decisions adopted by the entire membership convened as the Presidents Committee. The Technical Committee is composed of 16 members representing the larger, more developed and internationalized markets, and the EMC is composed of 56 members representing the emerging markets. In addition, IOSCO has constituted four Regional Standing Committees: the Africa/Middle-East Regional Committee, the Asia-Pacific Regional Committee, the European Regional Committee and the Interamerican Regional Committee. These Committees meet periodically to discuss matters specific to their respective regions.

Each member of an IOSCO Committee is represented by its Chairman or Chief Executive; the IOSCO consultative and decision making process therefore involves the top representatives of the world's securities regulators, from both the emerging markets and the more developed markets. IOSCO is supported by a small Secretariat based in Montreal, Canada, and the work of the Organization is conducted through the Committees and Working Groups (as described below) by senior and expert representatives of the member agencies.

The structure of IOSCO, combining global reach, participation by members at the highest level, and consensus-building, ensures that IOSCO's recommendations, guidelines and work product reflect global concerns, including those particular to emerging markets, and are accepted by virtually all of the world's securities regulators. This high level of consensus and support from the world-wide community of regulators is particularly important as it can provide the support that member agencies need to promote domestic legislative change. This role of IOSCO as a forum for promoting market integrity and investor confidence in individual domestic markets promotes financial stability world-wide.

III. Working to Meet the Needs of Emerging Securities Markets

The concerns and interests of regulators in emerging economies, and the need to foster sound regulatory systems, have always had a high priority in IOSCO's work agenda. This is reflected in IOSCO's broad mem-

Prepared for the G-10 Working Group on Financial Stability in Emerging Market Economies, Montreal, April 7, 1997.

bership structure, and the participation of both emerging and developed economies in all of IOSCO's work.

The structure and objectives of the EMC reflect IOSCO's commitment to the development of sound regulatory principles in emerging securities markets. The objectives of the EMC are:

- the development and improvement of the efficiency of emerging securities markets through the establishment of sound regulatory principles and minimum standards;
- the preparation of training programs for the personnel of members;
- the exchange of information; and
- the transfer of technology and expertise.

The EMC Steering Committee oversees the activities of the five EMC Working Groups. The EMC Steering Committee is made up of the EMC members that sit on the Executive Committee and the five Working Group Chairmen, and chaired by the Chairman of the EMC. Members meet and communicate on a regular basis during the year in order to ensure that the five Working Groups follow their mandated terms of reference and specific work programs as closely and as efficiently as possible.

The Technical Committee and the EMC have adopted parallel working group structures. The EMC Working Groups pursue their mandates in two parallel directions: (1) issues of specific interest to EMC members; and (2) issues being examined by the parallel Technical Committee Working Group. The Technical Committee and the EMC have also agreed to exchange observers on Working Groups in order to enhance practical cooperation. The EMC Working Group chairmen therefore receive and provide input from and to the Technical Committee Working Groups. This high degree of coordination and cooperation between the two Committees enables the EMC to better focus its resources on some of the practical difficulties specifically encountered by its members.

In addition to supporting the particular focus of the EMC, IOSCO continues to seek ways to incorporate the concerns and interests of regulators in emerging markets into the Organization as a whole. For example, IOSCO recently increased the representation of emerging markets regulators on the IOSCO Executive Committee and reinforced the importance of regional groupings within the formal structure of the Organization. This new structure has also enhanced the ability of IOSCO to address issues and make recommendations that are valid for both emerging and developed markets.

In addition, IOSCO is committed to long-term training for securities regulators from emerging markets. IOSCO is currently planning a new educational program, directed by the Secretary General and designed to facilitate the transfer of regulatory expertise within the Organization. The focus of the initial pro-

gram, expected to be held in September 1997, will be the regulation of financial intermediaries (in particular brokers and financial advisers) in emerging markets. By conducting a training program on the practical aspects of the licensing, regulation and inspection of broker-dealers and other market participants, IOSCO can foster more effective supervision of market intermediaries, and thereby contribute to market confidence and integrity.

For more than 10 years IOSCO has conducted an On-the-Job Training Program, in the course of which approximately sixty staff members of regulatory agencies from emerging markets have received training at member agencies in more developed markets. The On-the-Job Training Program provides a useful complement to the extensive inter-agency training programs that have been in place at IOSCO member agencies for many years and have contributed to the development of sound regulatory structures and practices for emerging markets.

IV. Working Groups and Coordination of Regulatory Initiatives

The structure of IOSCO results in a work product that is relevant to both developed and emerging markets. As described above, the EMC and the Technical Committee have adopted analogous working group structures with parallel overall mandates, and while the EMC Working Groups focus on issues specific to emerging markets, the Groups maintain a close liaison with their parallel groups in the other Committee. This structure fosters mutual awareness of issues and approaches, and allows IOSCO to speak with a unified voice. The five Working Groups of the Technical and Emerging Markets Committees are as follows:

A. Working Group No. 1 on Cross-Border Offerings and Listings:

Promoting the achievement of high, comparable, accounting, auditing and disclosure standards to facilitate cross-border securities offerings;

B. Working Group No. 2 on Regulation of Secondary Markets:

Promoting measures to enhance the transparency, integrity and robustness of financial markets and market processes;

C. Working Group No. 3 on Regulation of Financial Intermediaries:

Promoting the development of effective supervisory arrangements for securities firms and, in particular, for internationally active and diversified groups;

D. Working Group No. 4 on Enforcement and the Exchange of Information:

Promoting improved cooperation and communication among regulatory authorities, and contributing to the battle against international financial fraud;

E. Working Group No. 5 on Investment Management:

Promoting standards to facilitate the cross-border regulation of internationally marketed collective investment schemes ("CIS") and their fund managers.

V. Substantially All of IOSCO's Work Program and Regulatory Initiatives Are Intended to Foster Sound Regulatory Principles in Emerging and Developed Markets

IOSCO's work product takes many forms, including: member resolutions; recommendations for action; model guidelines; reports; and the promulgation of principles. Indeed, IOSCO has produced more than 40 reports and other documents which, taken together, embody comprehensive principles and guidelines for the regulation and supervision of securities and futures markets world-wide. Through their dissemination among the IOSCO membership, these principles and guidelines contribute in a very real and tangible way to the development of transparent markets, investor protection and financial stability. While, as described below and in the attached Appendix, specific work projects have focused on the particular interests of the emerging markets, all of IOSCO's work promotes high regulatory standards and strong markets throughout the world.

For the purposes of this memorandum, these initiatives have been organized under the seven key elements that are common to any sound securities regulatory regime. The common theme underlying each of these elements is the promotion and development of market integrity and investor confidence.

A. Measures Designed to Enhance the Authority of Securities Regulators to Act in a Timely and Objective Manner in Enforcing Securities Laws and Investigating Potential Violations

The dramatic growth of international financial operations has had a major impact on the work of securities regulators. In an age of borderless markets, regulators must work together internationally in order to be effective domestically. IOSCO has long stood for the importance of cooperation and assistance in enhancing the ability of regulators to enforce securities and futures laws and investigate potential violations. Through

the efforts of IOSCO, securities and futures regulators have established mechanisms to share information necessary to investigate cross-border frauds and permit the initiation of legal action against wrongdoers.

In 1994, IOSCO members reaffirmed their commitment to mutual assistance and cooperation by adopting a **Resolution on Commitment to Basic IOSCO Principles of High Regulatory Standards and Mutual Cooperation and Assistance**. Among other things, the resolution calls on each IOSCO member to conduct an evaluation of its own ability to collect and share information, including information about the beneficial ownership of bank and brokerage accounts. This self-evaluation process is currently under way. In addition, a task force consisting of the Chairmen of the Executive, Technical and Emerging Markets Committees has been formed to develop recommendations for building on the self-evaluations to encourage and improve international cooperation. Recommendations are expected to include strategies for enhancing information disclosure by under-regulated and uncooperative jurisdictions. IOSCO addressed the challenges presented by such jurisdictions in its *Report on Under-Regulated and Uncooperative Jurisdictions* (October 1994), in which it made a series of **recommendations for collective action**.

Given the ease with which funds can be transferred from one jurisdiction to another, and thereby out of the reach of defrauded investors, there is also a need for regulators to cooperate with one another in order to track and facilitate the recovery of funds across international borders. In this regard, IOSCO has issued **recommendations** relating to:

- adopting measures and mechanisms to deprive perpetrators of financial fraud of the proceeds of their activities;
- highlighting potential pathways for improvements in jurisdictions where there are few means to address the issue; and
- facilitating the return of the assets and interests of defrauded investors to their legitimate owners.

These recommendations are contained in an IOSCO report focusing on the means used by 27 different jurisdictions to protect the interests and assets of defrauded investors (*Measures Available on a Cross-Border Basis to Protect Interests and Assets of Defrauded Investors* (July 1996)).

In 1991, IOSCO promulgated ten **Principles for use by securities and futures regulatory authorities in developing MOUs with their foreign counterparts** (*Principles of Memoranda of Understanding* (September 1991)). These Principles have been incorporated into many of the more than 300 MOUs now in existence world-wide. The development of an extensive network of MOUs has resulted in greatly improved cooperation among regulators, contributing to the maintenance of safe and secure markets.

B. Establishing Clear Regulatory Responsibility for Licensing and Regulation of Securities Market Participants and Transactions, Including Reporting, Record Keeping, Inspection and Disciplinary Procedures

Clear, well-defined procedures for licensing and regulation of securities market participants and transactions are crucial to sound regulatory systems in both developed and emerging markets. In light of this principle the President's Committee adopted a **Resolution on International Conduct of Business Principles** setting out the basic standards of business conduct for financial firms. In adopting this resolution, IOSCO members underscored the importance of implementing and promoting these principles in their jurisdictions.

IOSCO has recognized that it is critical to the public confidence in financial markets that client assets be properly handled and accounted for. The threat to client assets is perhaps most acute when the firm is unable to compensate its clients for losses because it is facing insolvency. Therefore, IOSCO has published **twenty recommendations on measures and mechanisms that jurisdictions should establish as best practice to provide a high level of protection for assets and interests of clients held by financial intermediaries**. A self-assessment has been initiated to determine the level of compliance of IOSCO members with these recommendations. (*Report on Client Asset Protection* (August 1996)).

Procedures for the orderly disposition of a market default are a key component of any sound regulatory regime, and are essential to investor confidence. This is specially true in the dynamic area of futures and options transactions. IOSCO has affirmed the importance of transparency of market default procedures for providing certainty and predictability to market participants, facilitating orderly handling in the event of a default, and enabling market participants to make informed assessments. The issue has been addressed in three specific measures:

- the **publication of a list of information items that should be available to market participants** as to market default procedures regarding futures and options trading;
- a **recommendation on Communications upon Implementation of Default Procedures**;
- **recommendations for Best Practices on the Treatment of Positions, Funds and Assets in the Event of the Default of a Member Firm**. These recommendations are designed to permit prompt isolation of problems in order to minimize systemic risk.

All of the above can be found in the March 1996 report entitled *Default Procedures*.

IOSCO work in progress includes a report on the regulatory framework for short selling and securities lending by market intermediaries, which should help EMC members better address key regulatory issues in these areas.

Emerging markets are also addressing the challenges presented by the rapid growth in derivatives activities. In 1994 IOSCO published a set of **principles and guidelines for the development of derivatives markets in emerging markets**. These principles and guidelines deal with the conditions for the development and regulation of derivative markets, and the characteristics of an adequate financial infrastructure and market structure (*Report of the Development Committee Task Force on Derivatives* (September 1994)).

Following up on the 1994 Report, IOSCO published a set of **guidelines and recommendations on the appropriate regulatory approach for jurisdictions that are developing or plan to develop derivatives markets** (*Legal and Regulatory Framework for Exchange Traded Derivatives* (1996)). This Report makes use of reports from six emerging market agencies (Brazil, Chinese Taipei, Korea, Malaysia, South Africa and Thailand) that describe their experiences and plans in the area of derivative markets regulation. These analyses provide a useful reference for jurisdictions considering the development of derivatives markets.

It is worth mentioning in this context that the CVM of Brazil, a member of the EMC, has for the past two years offered Training Sessions on Practical Aspects of the Development and Operation of Derivatives Markets, directed to regulators from emerging economies.

IOSCO also has discussions in progress with the Bank for International Settlements ("BIS") Committee on Payment and Settlement Systems ("CPSS") regarding regulatory issues related to securities custody and lending.

C. Auditing, Accounting and Disclosure Standards for Securities Issuers, and Corporate Governance Standards to Ensure Protection and Enforcement of Shareholders Rights

One of IOSCO's most important initiatives is its coordination with the International Accounting Standards Committee ("IASC") as the IASC works to develop a core set of high-quality international accounting standards ("IAS"). In July 1995, IOSCO and the IASC agreed to a workplan that, upon successful completion, currently scheduled for March 1998, could result in IOSCO endorsement of IAS for use in cross-border capital raising and listing in global markets. IOSCO has been engaged in an intensive review and consultative process with the IASC, including attendance as an observer at IASC Board meetings, designed to promote progress on this undertaking.

IOSCO has begun an analysis of the work of the International Federation of Accountants ("IFAC") towards the development of acceptable International Standards for Audits ("ISA"). A comparison of certain of the ISAs to several national auditing standards has been initiated. The results of this work will be used to guide future substantive discussions with IFAC during 1997.

Additional IOSCO measures to improve disclosure standards include:

- development of **international standards for non-financial statements disclosures** for use by foreign issuers in cross-border offerings and listings;
- publication in 1994 of **recommendations for minimum disclosure standards for public securities offerings** and a *Model Prospectus for Emerging Markets;* and
- publication in 1996 of **guidelines for the reporting of material events by issuers of publicly traded securities in emerging markets** (*Reporting of Material Events*).

IOSCO work in progress includes standards for *Interim Reporting and Presentation of Financial Statements*.

D. Strengthening Enforcement of Laws and Regulations Against Fraud and Market Manipulation by Requiring the Establishment of Audit Trails with Respect to Trading, Clearance and Settlement Activities

IOSCO has devoted a substantial measure of attention and energy to promote sound, effective and efficient market processes. For example, in 1992 IOSCO published a detailed **blueprint for establishing or developing an efficient and risk-minimizing clearing and settlement system in emerging market economies** (*Clearing and Settlement in Emerging Markets: A Blueprint*). The blueprint uses the nine recommendations of the Group of Thirty (G-30) on clearing and settlement to frame the characteristics of an efficient clearing and settlement system, and goes on to discuss both the non-technical policy issues that must be addressed and the technical design questions. As a practical follow-up to this work, the Malaysian Securities Commission, a member of the EMC of IOSCO, will be holding a training session and an international seminar on clearing and settlement in emerging economies, on March 3–5, 1997, directed to regulators of emerging markets.

Another example of IOSCO initiatives in the area of clearing and settlement is the recent development, with the BIS's CPSS, of a disclosure framework for securities settlement. This framework will assist regulators and market participants in evaluating the risks associated with cross-border securities settlement.

IOSCO work in progress in this area also includes: (i) development of a legal framework to support the operations of central securities depositories and to offer a greater degree of legal certainty for partici-

pants; and (ii) a report, *Implications of the Use of Internet and Other Electronic Networks on the Regulation of Secondary Markets.*

E. Supervision of Market Intermediaries, Including the Establishment of Financial Responsibility Requirements

Effective supervision of market intermediaries is essential to the maintenance of just, efficient and sound markets. IOSCO continues to devote a great deal of effort and attention to this area, as demonstrated by the work product of the Technical Committee and EMC Working Parties on the Supervision of Market Intermediaries. In this regard, because IOSCO believes that close international cooperation is essential, it has continued to increase its cooperative activities with other regulatory groups as called for by the G-7 Ministers in their 1995 and 1996 Communiqués. Among other things, IOSCO and the Basle Committee have jointly established **eight major principles of supervision** which set out the overarching objectives of the supervision of market intermediaries. These principles are:

- cooperation and information flows among supervisory authorities should be as free as possible from impediments both nationally and internationally;
- all banks and securities firms should be subject to effective supervision, including the supervision of capital;
- geographically and/or functionally diversified financial groups require special supervisory arrangements;
- all banks and securities firms should have adequate capital;
- proper risk management by the firm is a prerequisite for financial stability;
- the transparency and integrity of markets and supervision rely on adequate reporting and disclosure of operations;
- the resilience of markets to the failure of individual firms must be maintained;
- the supervisory process needs to be constantly maintained and improved.

(*Joint Statement of IOSCO and the Basle Committee on Banking Supervision* (May 1996))

Other important initiatives taken by IOSCO to foster more effective supervision of market intermediaries include a survey on capital adequacy regimes for market intermediaries among members of the EMC, which is scheduled for completion during 1997. The EMC also expects to issue a report, during 1997, on *Financial Risk Management in Emerging Derivatives Markets,* which will review policies and actions taken by EMC members with respect to supervision of derivatives markets' risk management.

One of the key factors in the effective supervision of market intermediaries is the financial responsibility of market participants. IOSCO has taken several important initiatives in this field, especially on the topic of the management and mitigation of potential risks associated with derivatives positions. For example:

- the world-wide growth of the OTC derivatives business led to the adoption by IOSCO in March 1996 of a **recommendation on the *Recognition of Bilateral Netting Agreements in the Calculation of Capital Requirements for Securities Firms***. This recommendation takes note of the increasing importance of the OTC derivatives business as a proportion of the overall business of securities firms, and encourages the use of legally enforceable bilateral netting agreements by authorized securities firms;
- the growth in derivatives trading activity in the securities sector has prompted firms to develop methods to analyse, control and report their trading risk in a consistent and reliable way. Firms have increasingly been turning to more sophisticated quantitative based risk management methodologies using modern option and portfolio theory. This trend has led to the development of value at risk modelling techniques. The IOSCO Technical Committee is currently considering the appropriateness of the use of value at risk models by securities regulators for capital adequacy purposes and continues to cooperate with the Basle Committee on model testing and analysis. The basis for this consideration is the July 1995 report on the *Implications for Securities Regulators of the Increased Use of Value-at-Risk Models by Securities Firms*. This Report recognises the role played by value at risk models in improving internal controls and risk-based capital standards for securities firms. The Report explains how the value at risk models are constructed, points out the role that models should play as part of a firm's risk management procedures, and considers the implications for securities regulators of recognising the output of value at risk models for the purpose of calculating capital requirements for market risk.

IOSCO recognizes that supervisors should continuously improve their understanding of how exchange-traded and OTC derivatives affect the overall risk profile and profitability of market intermediaries. IOSCO and the Basle Committee have set out **guidelines for the types of information that regulators and supervisors should obtain from banks and securities firms in order to form a judgement as to the risks associated with proprietary and client-based derivative trading activities** (*Framework for Supervisory Information About the Derivatives Activities of Banks and Securities Firms* (May 1995)).

IOSCO and the Basle Committee have also jointly prepared a set of **recommendations for improved disclosure of both quantitative and qualitative information about derivative trading activities**. These recommendations are contained in *Public Disclosure of the Trading Activities of Banks and Securities Firms* (November 1995), which also reviews disclosure practices adopted by a large number of banks and securities firms in their 1994 annual accounts. An update to this report, including 1995 data, was released in November 1996.

F. Establishing Open, Transparent Stock Exchanges and Other Self-Regulatory Organizations ("SROs") for Market Participants, Which Are Subject to Oversight by the Securities Regulator

IOSCO is uniquely placed to foster international cooperation and information sharing between securities regulators. It is important that market authorities closely monitor exposures that are large enough to put the market at risk and share information with one another so as to manage market risk.

IOSCO has put forward some important **recommendations for cooperation between market authorities in the monitoring of and exchange of information on large exposures on futures and options markets**. IOSCO **recommends** that market authorities (regulatory bodies, SROs or the markets themselves) consider establishing trigger levels for open positions so that, when the trigger levels are reached, the beneficial owner of an open position can be identified. Given the increasing internationalization of trading activities, IOSCO also **recommends** that market authorities open and maintain channels of communication with one another in order to share information regarding large exposures. The recommendations propose the use of Information Sharing Arrangements between market authorities, and set forth the essential elements of such arrangements (*Cooperation Between Market Authorities* (March 1996)).

IOSCO work in progress includes the development of **guidelines for surveillance techniques and practices to detect and prosecute price manipulation**.

G. Establishing Standards of Regulation for Collective Investment Schemes

Collective Investment Schemes (CIS) are a rapidly growing sector of the securities business, and IOSCO has devoted a great deal of attention to CIS-related issues. CIS are of particular interest to emerging markets: they offer a flexible, simple and convenient means for investors, including small savers, to participate in domestic and international securities markets. The development of CIS can therefore increase both foreign and domestic investment in an emerging market. IOSCO has devoted significant time and attention to the development of sound regulatory principles for CIS, thereby contributing to the growth and stability of emerging markets.

IOSCO has recommended **core principles for the development and supervision of CIS**, focusing specifically on the needs of emerging markets regulators. These recommendations, contained in the recent IOSCO report, *Collective Investment Schemes,* provide guidance for the regulatory activities of EMC members. In order that emerging markets can apply solutions that best fit their own particular circumstances, the report also includes a comparative analysis of the CIS regulatory regimes in place in four EMC member jurisdictions.

International regulatory cooperation can be of critical importance to maintaining market integrity in emergencies involving the cross-border activity of CIS. These emergencies can take the forms of the insolvency or threatened insolvency of the CIS manager, trustee, custodian or affiliated company, or of a misappropriation of funds. The increased internationalization of the markets in which CIS and their principals operate can give these emergencies cross-border implications. Therefore, IOSCO has developed a set of **recommended policies for cooperation between regulators during an emergency**, and a set of **general principles for regulators to consider in the context of the suspension of dealing and marketing** (*Regulatory Cooperation in Emergencies* (June 1996)).

The increasing popularity of the CIS as an investment vehicle has also increased the need for disclosure of risk. Market integrity and investor protection hinge on the issue of accurate disclosure, and IOSCO has **recommended** a variety of ways of improving the presentation of risk factors in CIS offering documents and advertising, and proposed **policies** for ensuring that financial intermediaries adequately explain the risks of CIS investment to potential investors (*Disclosure of Risk—A Discussion Paper* (September 1996)).

Another category of risks to be addressed in the context of CIS are those risks regarding the custody of cash deposits and non-cash assets. The failure of a financial institution with responsibility for custody will have consequences for CIS regulators, supervising CIS and fund management entities alike. The increase in cross-border activity led IOSCO to issue **guidelines** on the subjects of contractual arrangements between a custodian and the operator of a CIS, including the selection and authorization of custodians, co-mingling of assets and omnibus accounts, and monitoring of custody arrangements. (*Guidance on Custody Arrangements for Collective Investment Schemes—A Discussion Paper* (September 1996)).

VI. Conclusion

The dramatic increase in securities transactions and the increasingly globalized marketplace has set new challenges for securities regulators world-wide. The members of IOSCO recognize that market integrity, investor protection and financial stability can only be achieved through a high level of cooperation and communication. IOSCO provides the forum for that cooperation and communication, allowing members to share their expertise, make concrete their commitment to the goals of market integrity and investor protection, provide practical assistance to other members, and supply critical leverage to regulators seeking to influence domestic legislation and regulation. IOSCO's commitment to these goals, accompanied by its global reach, participation by members at the highest level, and consensus-building have enabled IOSCO to make important contributions to the development of sound securities regulatory principles in both emerging and developed markets.

APPENDIX

Activities of the EMC Working Groups

EMC activities, particularly those of its Working Groups, have strengthened the cooperation between its members and have contributed to the development of an integrated approach for the development of standards for improving the transparency of emerging securities and futures markets.

A. Working Group No. 1: Disclosure and Accounting

In coordination with the Working Group No. 1 of the Technical Committee, the Working Group is addressing the development of standards to facilitate multi-jurisdictional securities offerings, which take into account the market experiences and particularities of EMC members. It is also working towards developing a set of recommendations of Interim Reporting in relation to *"Presentation of Financial Statements"*. In its last meeting, the EMC approved the report entitled *"Reporting Material Events"*.

B. Working Group No. 2: Regulation of Secondary Markets

This Working Group has a specific mandate to develop a legal and regulatory framework for cash and derivative markets in emerging jurisdictions.

A Report entitled *"The Legal and Regulatory Framework for Exchange Traded Derivatives"* was made public at IOSCO's most recent Annual Conference and serves as a very useful reference document for jurisdictions considering the development of derivatives markets. The report encompasses the following issues and regulatory objectives:

- Market Integrity and Efficiency: Product Design, Order Execution; Surveillance and Operational Capacity;

- Financial Safety and Integrity: Capital Standards; Clearing Facility; Margins; Protection of Customers Funds; Default, Insolvency of Bankruptcy Provisions, Market Disruptions;
- Customer Protection and Fairness: Automation/Registration/Licensing; Order Execution; Record Keeping; Sales Representation and Disclosure; Product Design; Dispute Resolution Programs;
- Compliance and Enforcement.

The EMC has also authorized the Working Group to develop a legal framework to support the operations of central securities depositories and to offer a greater degree of legal certainty to participants. Two other mandates relate to financial risk management in emerging derivatives markets and transparency relating to block trading.

C. Working Group No. 3: Regulation of Market Intermediaries

This Working Group has a specific mandate to identify the objectives and criteria of capital adequacy standards enforced in the jurisdictions of EMC members along with the type of risks involved. It is also developing a comparative analysis of the regulatory approaches used by EMC members, including a description of regulatory issues in the area of the regulation of market intermediaries. The Working Group is planning to design a capital adequacy regime for jurisdictions represented within the EMC, which would use a variable approach depending on the level of development of capital markets and, in particular, the degree of sophistication of the financial instruments used.

The EMC gave the Working Group a new mandate pertaining to short selling and securities lending by market intermediaries and has also asked the Working Group to assist its Technical Committee Working Party counterpart in the preparation of a self-evaluation questionnaire to determine the level of implementation by IOSCO members of the recommendations contained in the Technical Committee report on *Client Asset Protection.*

D. Working Group No. 4: Enforcement and the Exchange of Information

Working Group No. 4 has a specific mandate to create conditions for improving and sharing enforcement expertise among EMC members. It is encouraging the efforts of EMC members to combat international securities fraud, and at the same time is working on the identification of principles of securities regulation in areas such as the organization of regulatory and supervisory systems, and the investigation and enforcement powers of supervisory authorities. The Working Group drafted the two Resolutions adopted by the EMC in September 1996, namely *"Proposal of Recommendation on Standard Catalogue of Illicit Activities to be Recognized and Penalized on the Securities Markets"* and *"Proposal of Recommendation on the Enforcement Powers of a Securities and Futures Markets Supervisory Agency."*

It has also started work on its mandate relating to the development of guidelines for surveillance techniques and practices for detecting and prosecuting, for law enforcement purposes, price manipulation on the securities markets.

At its most recent meeting, the EMC approved a report entitled *"Discussion Paper on Class Action or Other Provisions Designed to Protect the Interest of Defrauded Investors in Civil Proceedings."*

E. Working Group No. 5: Investment Management

EMC Working Group No. 5 has a specific mandate to determine regulatory objectives for the promotion and supervision of investment management services and to structure an appropriate regulatory framework for EMC members that would take into consideration high, medium or low intensity regulation.

The Working Group also has to evaluate the role of the regulatory authorities and to prepare a comparative analysis of the different systems used for the promotion or development of investment management services in developed as well as emerging markets.

The EMC recently approved a Report entitled *"Collective Investment Schemes"* which concentrates on the needs of emerging markets regulators pertaining to the regulations of CIS. The Report also embodies basic principles for the development and supervision of CIS and also includes a comparative analysis of the CIS regulatory regimes in 4 EMC countries.

The Working Group plans also to address issues relating to cross-border marketing of CIS.

References

Alexander, William E., Jeffrey M. Davis, Liam P. Ebrill, and Carl-Johan Lindgren, 1997, *Systemic Bank Restructuring and Macroeconomic Policy* (Washington: International Monetary Fund).

Bagehot, Walter, 1873, *Lombard Street: A Description of the Money Market* (New York: Scribner, Armstrong; Reprinted, Homewood, Illinois: Dow Jones, 1962).

Basle Committee on Banking Supervision, 1975, *Report on the Supervision of Banks' Foreign Establishments* (Basle: Bank for International Settlements).

———, 1983, *Principles for the Supervision of Banks' Foreign Establishments* (Basle: Bank for International Settlements).

———, 1988a, *International Convergence of Capital Measurement and Capital Standards* (Basle: Bank for International Settlements).

———, 1988b, *Prevention of Criminal Use of the Banking System for the Purpose of Money-Laundering* (Basle: Bank for International Settlements).

———, 1991, *Measuring and Controlling Large Credit Exposures* (Basle: Bank for International Settlements).

———, 1992, *Minimum Standards for the Supervision of International Banking Groups and Their Cross-border Establishments* (Basle: Bank for International Settlements).

———, 1993, *Case Study of the Insolvency and Liquidation of a Multinational Bank* (Basle: Bank for International Settlements).

———, 1995a, *Framework for Supervisory Information about the Derivatives Activities of Banks and Securities Firms,* issued jointly with IOSCO (Basle: Bank for International Settlements).

———, 1995b, *Public Disclosure of the Trading and Derivatives Activities of Banks and Securities Firms* (Basle: Bank for International Settlements).

———, 1996a, *Amendment to the Basle Capital Accord to Incorporate Market Risks* (Basle: Bank for International Settlements).

———, 1996b, *Survey of Disclosures About Trading and Derivatives Activities of Banks and Securities Firms,* issued jointly with IOSCO (Basle: Bank for International Settlements).

———, 1996c, *The Supervision of Cross-Border Banking* (Basle: Bank for International Settlements).

———, 1997a, *Discussion Paper on Principles for the Management of Interest Rate Risk* (Basle: Bank for International Settlements).

———, 1997b, *Compendium of Documents* (Basle: Bank for International Settlements).

———, 1997c, *Core Principles for Effective Banking Supervision* (Basle: Bank for International Settlements).

Beattie, Vivien, et al., 1995, *Banks and Bad Debts, Accounting for Loan Losses in International Banking* (Chichester: John Wiley and Sons).

CEMLA, 1992, "Propuesta Para La Evaluación De Los Activos Crediticios De Las Instituciones De Intermediación Financiera," in *Octava Asamblea de la Comisión de Organismos de Supervisión y Fiscalización Bancaria de América Latina y el Caribe* (México).

Committee on Payment and Settlement Systems, 1996, *Settlement Risk in Foreign Exchange Transactions* (Basle: Bank for International Settlements).

Comptroller of the Currency, 1991, Quarterly Journal, Volume 15 (March), pp. 77-81.

Dziobek, Claudia, Olivier Frécaut, and Maria Nieto, 1995, "Non-G-10 Countries and the Basle Capital Rules: How Tough a Challenge Is It to Join the Basle Club?" IMF Paper on Policy Analysis and Assessment 95/5 (Washington: International Monetary Fund).

Euro-currency Standing Committee, 1994, *Public Disclosure of Market and Credit Risks by Financial Intermediaries* (Fisher Report) (Basle: Bank for International Settlements).

———, 1996, *Proposals for Improving Global Derivatives Market Statistics* (Basle: Bank for International Settlements).

European Union Council, 1977, "Directive on the coordination of the laws, regulations and administrative provisions relating to the taking up and pursuit of the business of credit institutions" (77/780/EEC), *Official Journal of the European Communities,* No. L 322/30 (Brussels: European Union).

———, 1986, "Directive on the annual accounts and consolidated accounts of banks and other financial institutions" (86/635/EEC), *Official Journal of the European Communities,* No. L 372/1 (Brussels: European Union).

———, 1989, "Directive on the coordination of laws, regulations and administrative provisions relating to the taking up and pursuit of the business of credit institutions and amending Directive 77/780/EEC" (89/646/EEC), *Official Journal of the European Communities,* No. L 386/1 (Brussels: European Union).

———, 1991, "Directive on the prevention of use of the financial system for the purpose of money laundering" (91/308/EEC), *Official Journal of the European Communities,* No. L 166/77 (Brussels: European Union).

———, 1992a, "Directive on the supervision of credit institutions on a consolidated basis" (92/30/EEC), *Official Journal of the European Communities,* No. L 110/52 (Brussels: European Union).

———, 1992b, "Directive on monitoring and controlling large exposures of credit institutions" (92/121/EEC), *Official Journal of the European Communities,* No. L 29/1 (Brussels: European Union).

European Union Parliament and Council, 1995, "Directive amending Directives 77/780/EEC and 89/646/EEC in the field of credit institutions . . . with a view to reinforcing prudential supervision" (95/26/EC), *Official Journal of the European Communities,* No. L 168/7 29 (Brussels: European Union).

Financial Action Task Force, 1990, *Report on Money Laundering* (Paris: Financial Action Task Force).

Folkerts-Landau, David, and Takatoshi Ito, 1995 and 1996, *International Capital Markets—Developments, Prospects, and Key Policy Issues,* World Economic and Financial Surveys (Washington: International Monetary Fund).

Folkerts-Landau, David, Peter Garber, and Dirk Schoenmaker, 1996, "The Reform of Wholesale Payments Systems and Its Impact on Financial Markets," IMF Working Paper 96/37 (Washington: International Monetary Fund, April).

Folkerts-Landau, David, and Peter Garber, 1997, "International Derivative Markets and Financial System Soundness," paper presented at the International Monetary Fund Conference on Banking Soundness and Monetary Policy in a World of Global Capital Markets, Washington, January.

Garber, Peter M., 1996, "Managing Risks to Financial Markets from Volatile Capital Flows: The Role of Prudential Regulation," *International Journal of Finance and Economics,* Volume 1 (July), pp. 183–95.

Garcia, Gillian G., 1996, "Deposit Insurance: Obtaining the Benefits and Avoiding the Pitfalls," IMF Working Paper 96/83 (Washington: International Monetary Fund, August).

Goldstein, Morris, 1996, *The Case for an International Banking Standard* (Washington: International Institute of Economics).

Goodfriend, Marvin, and Robert G. King, 1988, "Financial Deregulation, Monetary Policy, and Central Banking," in *Restructuring Banking and Financial Services in America,* ed. by William S. Haraf and Rose Marie Kushmeider (Washington: American Enterprise Institute).

Greenspan, Alan, 1997, remarks at the meeting of the Institute of International Finance, Washington, April 29.

Group of Seven Heads of State and Government, 1996, *Economic Communiqué* (Lyon: G-7).

———, 1997, *Statement by the Group of Seven Heads of State and Government* (Denver: G-7).

Group of Ten, 1997, *Financial Stability in Emerging Market Economies: A strategy for the formulation, adoption, and implementation of sound principles and practices to strengthen financial systems.* A report of a working party, comprising representatives of the Group of Ten countries and emerging market economies.

Group of Thirty, Global Derivation Study Group, 1993, *Derivatives: Practices and Principles* (Washington: Group of Thirty).

———1996, *International Insolvencies in the Financial Sector,* Discussion Draft, in cooperation with INSOL International (Washington: Group of Thirty).

———1997, *Global Institutions, National Supervision and Systemic Risk* (Washington: Group of Thirty).

Hartmann, Philipp, 1995, "Capital Adequacy and Foreign Exchange Risk Regulation: Recent Developments in Industrial Countries," Special Paper No. 77 (London: London School of Economics Financial Markets Group).

International Accounting Standards Committee, 1995, *International Accounting for Financial Assets and Financial Liabilities* (Rochester, England: Stanhope Press).

———, 1994a, "Disclosures in the Financial Statements of Banks and Similar Financial Institutions," IAS 30 (London).

———, 1994b, "Financial Instruments: Disclosure and Presentation," IAS 32 (London).

International Monetary Fund, 1996, "Communiqué of the Interim Committee of the Board of Governors of the International Monetary Fund," PR/96/49 (September 29, 1996).

———, 1993, *System of National Accounts* (Washington: IMF).

Lindgren, Carl-Johan, Gillian Garcia, and Alexander Kiyei, *Deposit Insurance: Best Practices and Country Experiences,* IMF Occasional Paper (forthcoming).

Lindgren, Carl-Johan, Gillian Garcia, and Matthew Saal, 1996, *Bank Soundness and Macroeconomic Policy* (Washington: International Monetary Fund).

Pecchioli, R.M., 1987, *Prudential Supervision in Banking* (Paris: Organization for Economic Cooperation and Development).

Scott, David H., 1994, "The Regulation and Supervision of Domestic Financial Conglomerates," Policy Research Working Paper 1329 (Washington: World Bank, Financial Sector Development Department).

Tripartite Group of Bank, Securities and Insurance Regulators, 1995, *The Supervision of Financial Conglomerates* (Basle: Bank for International Settlements).

Tuya, José, and Lorena Zamalloa, 1994, "Issues on Placing Banking Supervision in the Central Bank," in *Frameworks for Monetary Stability,* ed. by Tomás J. Baliño and Carlo Cottarelli (Washington: International Monetary Fund).

Working Party on Financial Stability in Emerging Market Economies, 1997, *Financial Stability in Emerging Market Economies: A Strategy for the Formulation, Adoption, and Implementation of Sound Principles and Practices to Strengthen Financial Systems* (Basle: Bank for International Settlements).

World Bank, Financial Policy and Systems Division, 1992, *Bank Supervision Guidelines,* Nos. 6 and 13 (Washington: World Bank).

World Economic and Financial Surveys

This series (ISSN 0258-7440) contains biannual, annual, and periodic studies covering monetary and financial issues of importance to the global economy. The core elements of the series are the *World Economic Outlook* report, usually published in May and October, and the annual report on *International Capital Markets*. Other studies assess international trade policy, private market and official financing for developing countries, exchange and payments systems, export credit policies, and issues discussed in the *World Economic Outlook*. Please consult the IMF *Publications Catalog* for a complete listing of currently available World Economic and Financial Surveys.

World Economic Outlook: A Survey by the Staff of the International Monetary Fund

The *World Economic Outlook,* published twice a year in English, French, Spanish, and Arabic, presents IMF staff economists' analyses of global economic developments during the near and medium term. Chapters give an overview of the world economy; consider issues affecting industrial countries, developing countries, and economies in transition to the market; and address topics of pressing current interest.

ISSN 0256-6877.
$36.00 (academic rate: $25.00); paper.
1997 (Dec.). ISBN 1-55775-714-3 (English only). **Stock #WEO-1797.**
1997 (Oct.). ISBN 1-55775-681-3. **Stock #WEO-297.**
1997 (May). ISBN 1-55775-648-1. **Stock #WEO-197.**
1996 (Oct.). ISBN 1-55775-610-4. **Stock #WEO-296.**

International Capital Markets: Developments, Prospects, and Key Policy Issues
by an IMF staff team led by David Folkerts-Landau with Donald J. Mathieson and Garry J. Schinasi

This year's capital markets report provides a comprehensive survey of recent developments and trends in the mature and emerging capital markets, including equities, bonds, foreign exchange, and derivatives, and banking systems. It focuses on the implications of European Economic and Monetary Union (EMU) for financial markets and the management of external liabilities of emerging market countries.

$25.00 (academic rate: $20.00); paper.
1997. ISBN 1-55775-686-4. **Stock #WEO-697.**
1996. ISBN 1-55775-609-0. **Stock #WEO-696.**
1995. ISBN 1-55775-516-7. **Stock #WEO-695.**

Issues in International Exchange and Payments Systems
by a staff team from the IMF's Monetary and Exchange Affairs Department

The global trend toward liberalization in countries' international exchange and payments systems has been widespread in both industrial and developing countries and most dramatic in Central and Eastern Europe. Countries in general have brought their exchange systems more in line with market principles and moved toward more flexible exchange rate arrangements in recent years.

$25.00 (academic rate: $20.00); paper.
1995. ISBN 1-55775-480-2. **Stock #WEO-895.**

Staff Studies for the World Economic Outlook
by the IMF's Research Department

These studies, supporting analyses and scenarios of the *World Economic Outlook*, provide a detailed examination of theory and evidence on major issues currently affecting the global economy.

$25.00 (academic rate: $20.00); paper.
1997. ISBN 1-55775-701-1. **Stock #WEO-397.**
1995. ISBN 1-55775-499-3. **Stock #WEO-395.**

Private Market Financing for Developing Countries
by a staff team from the IMF's Policy Development and Review Department led by Steven Dunaway

The latest study surveys recent trends in flows to developing countries through banking and securities markets. It also analyzes the institutional and regulatory framework for developing country finance; institutional investor behavior and pricing of developing country stocks; and progress in commercial bank debt restructuring in low-income countries.

$25.00 (academic rate: $20.00); paper.
1995. ISBN 1-55775-526-4. **Stock #WEO-1595.**
1995. ISBN 1-55775-456-X. **Stock #WEO-995.**

Official Financing for Developing Countries
by a staff team in the IMF's Policy Development and Review Department led by Anthony R. Boote and Doris C. Ross

This study provides information on official financing for developing countries, with the focus on low-income countries. It updates the 1995 edition and reviews developments in direct financing by official and multilateral sources.

$25.00 (academic rate: $20.00); paper.
1998. ISBN 1-55775-702-X. **Stock #WEO-1397.**
1995. ISBN 1-55775-527-2. **Stock #WEO-1395.**
1994. ISBN 1-55775-702-378-4. **Stock #WEO-1394.**

Toward a Framework for Financial Stability
by a staff team led by David Folkerts-Landau and Carl-Johan Lindgren

This study outlines the broad principles and characteristics of stable and sound financial systems, to facilitate IMF surveillance over banking sector issues of macroeconomic significance and to contribute to the general international effort to reduce the likelihood and diminish the intensity of future financial sector crises.

$25.00 (academic rate: $20.00); paper.
1998. ISBN 1-55775-706-2. **Stock #WEO-016.**

Available by series subscription or single title (including back issues); academic rate available only to full-time university faculty and students. For earlier ediitons please inquire about prices.

The IMF *Catalog of Publications* is available on-line at the Internet address listed below.

Please send orders and inquiries to:
International Monetary Fund, Publication Services, 700 19th Street, N.W.
Washington, D.C. 20431, U.S.A.
Tel.: (202) 623-7430   Telefax: (202) 623-7201
E-mail: publications@imf.org
Internet: http://www.imf.org